T-6 TEXAN

in action

By Larry Davis

Color by Don Greer
Illustrated by Perry Manley

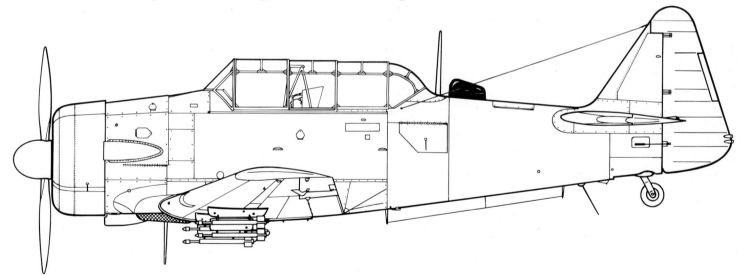

Aircraft Number 94

squadron/signal publications

NIGHT TRAIN, an LT-6G (49-3542) of the 6148th Tactical Air Control Squadron (Airborne), leads a flight of F-84G Thunderjets against Chinese positions along the Korean Main Line of Resistance during 1953.

ISBN 0-89747-224-1

If you have any photographs of the aircraft, armor, soldiers or ships of any nation, particularly wartime snapshots, why not share them with us and help make Squadron/Signal's books all the more interesting and complete in the future. Any photograph sent to us will be copied and the original returned. The donor will be fully credited for any photos used. Please send them to:

Squadron/Signal Publications, Inc.
1115 Crowley Drive.
Carrollton, TX 75011-5010.

Acknowledgements

Air Force Museum
Peter Bowers
Bob Dorr
Larry Hill
John Kirk
Dave Menard
North American Aviation
Smithsonian Institution
Norm Taylor

G. Avila
W. Cleveland
Don Garrett, Jr.
Imperial War Museum
Bill Larkins
Mosquito Association
RCAF
Dick Starinchak
U.S. Air Force

Dedication

This book is dedicated to all aircraft buffs throughout the world. Without the help of individuals like David Menard, Bill Larkins, Norm Taylor, Don Garrett, Bob Dorr, and others, no book on aviation history could be written and called complete or correct.

The T-6 Texan was the world's most widely produced trainer aircraft and was known to many as — The Pilot Maker. This pair of Air Force Reserve T-6Cs were based at Hamilton Field during August of 1947 and have the engine cowlings painted in Black and White. (Balogh)

INTRODUCTION

Whether you called it the Texan, Harvard, Yale, J-Bird, Mosquito, or simply the T-6, the North American T-6 trainer was one of the most important aircraft designs of the Second World War era — perhaps of all time. The North American Texan was built in greater numbers than most of the aircraft that it trained pilots for, or against! There were 17,096 Texans built by North American Aviation and the foreign companies that built the Texan under license overseas. This figure does not count the aircraft that were re-manufactured from existing airframes, or aircraft that used T-6 technology (P-64, NA-50, Boomerang) as their basis.

Although designed as a basic training aircraft, the T-6 would be used extensively in a number of other roles including: advanced trainer, fighter, interceptor, fighter-bomber, forward air control aircraft, and counter-insurgency (COIN) aircraft. The Texan was widely exported and served with at least fifty-five air forces throughout the world. In civilian hands it was used as a pylon racer, sport aircraft, mail carrier, and even as an airliner. The Texan served in all three of the modern era conflicts — World War II, Korea, and Vietnam. The Texan also saw action in dozens of brush-fire wars around the world including Algeria, the Congo, Biafra, the Middle East, and throughout Latin America.

Despite its impressive war record, the Texan is best known as a trainer. There have been a great many other aircraft developed for the trainer role; however, only the T-6 Texan is known by the name, PILOT MAKER.

North American Aviation began life during 1928 as a holding company for several other prominent American aviation firms. Initially North American owned large shares of companies like Curtiss Aircraft Corporation, Sperry, and airlines such as TWA. North American Aviation produced no designs of their own. They simply funded other companies and their designs; however, this all changed during 1933.

During 1933, North American Aviation was reorganized, and a new president was appointed. The new president was James "Dutch" Kindelberger, who had previously been the Chief Engineer at Douglas Aircraft Corp. He brought with him John Leland "Lee" Atwood. Together they created the manufacturing division of North American Aviation, known as the General Aviation Corporation, with production facilities located at the old Curtiss-Caproni plant in Dandalk, Maryland. The first aircraft to be designed by the two men was the General Aviation model 15 (GA-15), an observation aircraft intended for the U.S. Army Air Corps. The design was accepted by the Army, which ordered the aircraft into production as the O-47.

With the success of the O-47, Kindelberger and Atwood decided to try to win the 1934 Army Basic Trainer contract. This aircraft would be the first to carry the North American Aviation name. The North American trainer design, factory coded NA-16, was a blend of the traditional, and the innovative. The fuselage was traditional in that it was a steel tube frame covered with fabric. However, it differed in that it was built in sub-assemblies; the engine area, cockpit, upper rear fuselage, and under rear fuselage were all separate assemblies which were bolted together. Another innovation was the use of fabric covered access panels for easy maintenance of virtually any portion of the fuselage. The cockpits were traditional open types with small windscreens mounted in front of each. The aircraft was powered by a 400 hp Wright R-975-E7 Whirlwind nine cylinder air cooled radial engine.

The fuselage was mated to an all-metal, flush riveted, stressed-skin wing which bore a great resemblance to the wing found on the Douglas DC-1/DC-2 airliner (this was understandable since both men had formerly worked for Douglas). The forty-two foot

James H. 'Dutch' Kindelberger, Chairman of North American Aviation and designer of the T-6 series. (NAA)

wing was a three piece design similar to the DC-2 in that it had two outer wing panels bolted to a constant-chord center section. The flap design was also similar to the DC-2 with a large full span flap on the wing center section and split flaps on each outer wing panel. The amount of sweep to the outer wing panel leading and trailing edges and the wing dihedral angle was the same as the DC-2, with only the wing area being different.

The landing gear was a fixed single oleo leg mounted near the leading edge of the wing center section. Although the vertical and horizontal stabilizers were stressed-skin aluminum, all control surfaces were fabric covered. Since the NA-16 was intended to be a basic trainer aircraft, no provisions for armament were included in the design specifications.

The NA-16 was rolled out and flew for the first time on 1 April 1935, when company test pilot Eddie Allen lifted the Blue and Yellow trainer, marked with a civil serial, X-2080, off the Dandalk runway. This first flight was made just six weeks after the initial design specifications were submitted to the Army and had received its approval. The Army Basic Trainer Competition was held at Wright Field, Ohio, later that same month and the NA-16 prototype easily won the competition.

The Army, however, ordered several changes made to the prototype before the aircraft entered production. The cockpit area was to be fully enclosed with a sliding canopy, the landing gear had to have streamlined fairings installed over the struts and removable wheel pants over the wheels, the carburetor air intake was to be enlarged, and the inner to outer wing flange had to have a half-round cover installed over it. Once these changes were accomplished the Army inspected the prototype (now redesignated the NA-18) and ordered forty-two aircraft under the designation Basic Trainer type 9 — BT-9.

With the orders for the BT-9 and the O-47, North American was forced to seek new facilities to meet their expanded production needs. North American Aviation relocated to Inglewood, California in a brand new and greatly expanded factory where production of the BT-9 trainer got underway.

The North American NA-16 prototype featured open cockpits and fixed landing gear, which were traditional for Army basic trainers. The NA-16 prototype, registered X-2080, won the Army's 1935 Basic Trainer Competition. (NAA)

Before the NA-16 went into production, the Army specified several changes including an enclosed cockpit, faired landing gear legs, and wheel pants. The reconfigured prototype rolled out of the North American facility painted in the Army trainer color scheme which consisted of a Blue fuselage and Yellow wings. (AFM)

Prototype Development

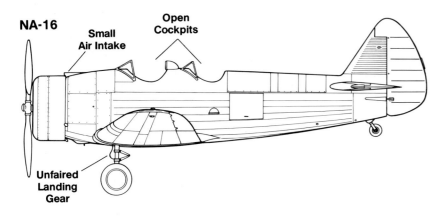

NA-16

Small Air Intake
Open Cockpits
Unfaired Landing Gear

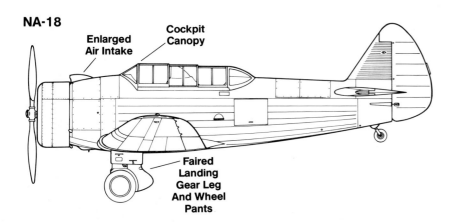

NA-18

Enlarged Air Intake
Cockpit Canopy
Faired Landing Gear Leg And Wheel Pants

Developments

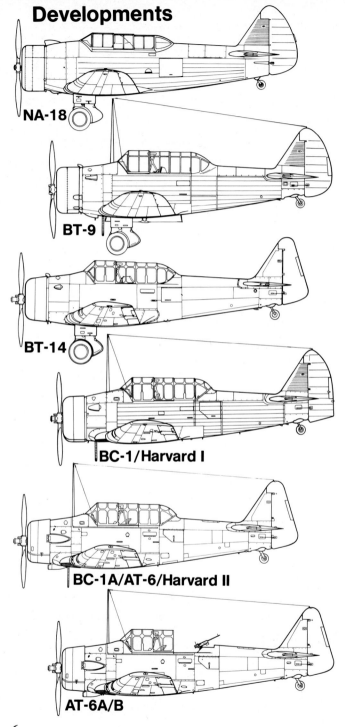

NA-18

BT-9

BT-14

BC-1/Harvard I

BC-1A/AT-6/Harvard II

AT-6A/B

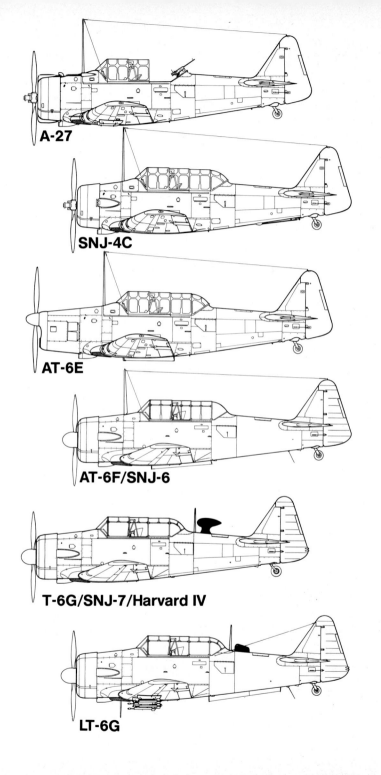

A-27

SNJ-4C

AT-6E

AT-6F/SNJ-6

T-6G/SNJ-7/Harvard IV

LT-6G

BT-9/NJ-1

The addition of the cockpit canopy, along with the other Army specified changes, led North American to change the factory code of the revised NA-16 to NA-18. In addition to the Army specified changes, North American made provisions for re-engining the NA-18 with a 600 hp Pratt & Whitney R-1340 Wasp engine. Additionally they also added provisions for armament: two .30 caliber machine guns mounted in the cowling and a single .30 caliber machine gun on a flexible mount in the rear cockpit. These later two changes, however, were not accepted by the Army for production BT-9s.

The U.S. Army was not the only one interested in the NA-18, and North American officials were actively attempting to sell the aircraft to other nations. As an export aircraft, the NA-18 was being marketed as a general purpose aircraft rather than just a trainer aircraft. The more powerful engine and armament remained as options that could be easily fitted to export NA-18s.

The production BT-9, factory coded NA-19, was powered by a 400 hp Wright R-975-7 Whirlwind engine driving a two blade propeller. With a gross weight of 3,860 pounds the BT-9 had a top speed of 175 mph, cruising speed of 155 mph, and a range of 810 miles. The rate of climb was 1,051 feet/minute and the service ceiling was 19,000 feet. The BT-9 introduced three significant items to Army trainer aircraft; a sliding cockpit canopy, flaps, and leading edge slats. The latter two items were a first for an Army trainer. The leading edge slats were not installed initially and were added later to the outer wing leading edges after tests with early production BT-9s revealed that the aircraft had bad wingtip stall characteristics.

The first production BT-9 was flown on 15 April 1936 and, to improve headroom for the crew, featured a taller cockpit canopy than the one that had been fitted to the prototype. Deliveries of production BT-9s, painted in the standard Blue and Yellow Army trainer colors, began during the Spring of 1936. Initially the Army ordered forty-two BT-9s; however, the Army quickly placed a follow-on order for forty modified BT-9s under the designation BT-9A. The BT-9A differed from the BT-9 in having five inches added to the

This BT-9 was assigned to the Army Air Corps flight school at Randolph Field, Texas, the "West Point of the Air", during 1939. The BT-9 differed from the prototype in having a taller canopy, different engine, revised cowling, and provisions for armament. (Louis Proper)

fuselage length. Initial production aircraft had the wing leading edge slats; however, these were replaced by a redesigned outer wing leading edge with a two degree washout being built in to solve the BT-9's wingtip stall characteristics. These changes were both attempts to increase the aircraft's stability.

With the BT-9A the Army also took up the armament option, ordering that these aircraft be armed with a single .30 caliber machine gun mounted in the starboard side of the cowling and a second .30 caliber gun in the rear cockpit on a flexible mount. Provisions were also made for gun cameras in both locations. The BT-9B followed with only minor changes that included a fixed rear canopy section and no armament. The Army purchased 117 BT-9Bs during 1937, followed by an order for sixty-seven BT-9Cs. The BT-9C was basically an improved BT-9A and was intended for use by the Organized Reserve Forces.

NJ-1

The U.S. Navy, in search for a high-performance instrument trainer with an enclosed cockpit, became interested in the BT-9 early in its development. One of the drawbacks to securing a Navy contract, however, was its engine. The Wright R-975 was not used in any Naval aircraft and the Navy desired an engine that was already in the Navy inventory. To meet this requirement, North American mated a 500 hp Pratt & Whitney R-1340 Wasp engine on the first production BT-9C airframe, using the company number NA-28 and Army experimental designation Y1BT-10 (later re-designated BT-10). The Navy quickly approved the combination and ordered forty aircraft under the designation NJ-1 (N for Trainer aircraft, J for North American, and -1 for the first aircraft from North American in this category).

The NJ-1 was basically an unarmed BT-9B powered by a 500 hp R-1340-6 Wasp engine and having a revised cowling. The airscoop on the top of the fuselage just behind the cowling was relocated to under the cowling on the NJ-1 and the engine exhaust stacks were relocated lower and further to the rear of the cowling. Deliveries of production NJ-1s commenced in July of 1937 with the NJ-1s being delivered to Navy training facilities such as Corry Field, Florida. The aircraft were delivered from the factory in the standard Navy trainer scheme of overall Aluminum dope with Orange-Yellow wing upper surfaces. Instrument trainers were marked with wide Red bands painted around the fuselage and wings. None of the NJ-1s were armed or fitted with tail hooks.

Canopy

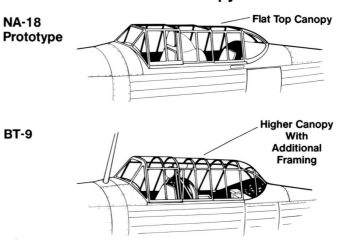

NA-18 Prototype

Flat Top Canopy

BT-9

Higher Canopy With Additional Framing

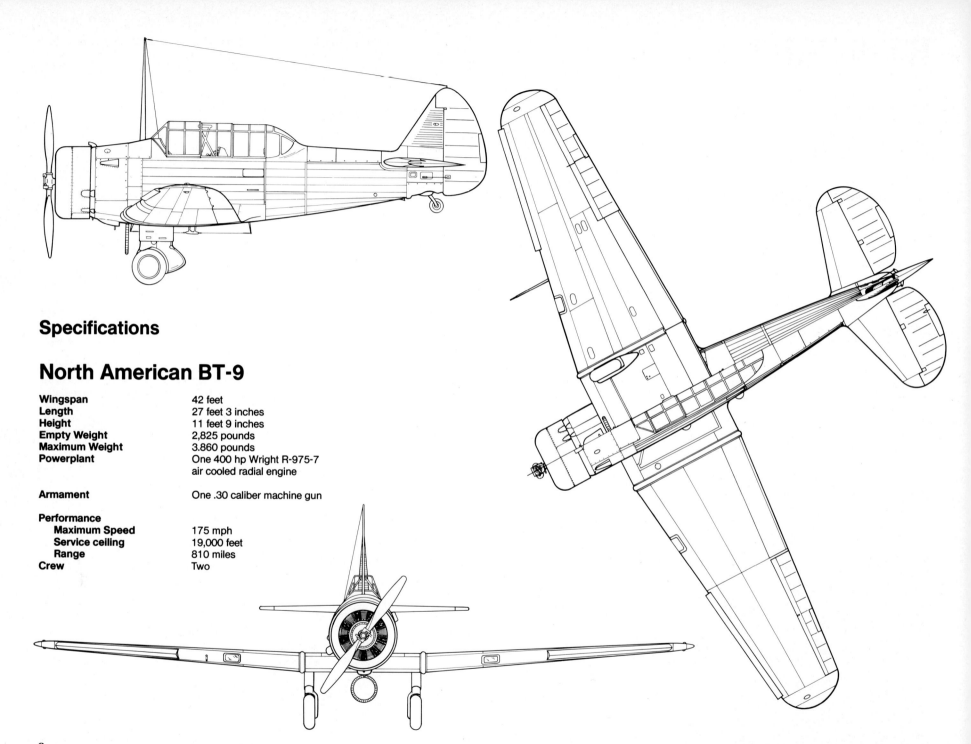

Specifications

North American BT-9

Wingspan	42 feet
Length	27 feet 3 inches
Height	11 feet 9 inches
Empty Weight	2,825 pounds
Maximum Weight	3.860 pounds
Powerplant	One 400 hp Wright R-975-7 air cooled radial engine
Armament	One .30 caliber machine gun
Performance	
Maximum Speed	175 mph
Service ceiling	19,000 feet
Range	810 miles
Crew	Two

The Army Air Corps normally assigned a BT-9 to each operational unit for pilot proficiency training. This BT-9 of the 30th Bomb Squadron, 19th Bomb Group has the cowling painted Blue, the fuselage Gloss Olive Green, and the wings and tail in Yellow-Orange. (Taylor)

Leading Edge Slats

BT-9 (Early)

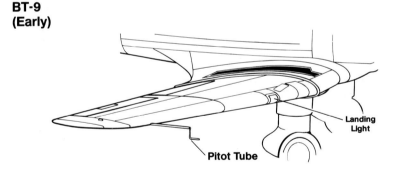

Landing Light

Pitot Tube

BT-9 (Late)
BT-9A (Early)

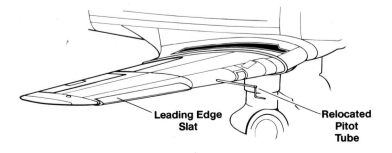

Leading Edge Slat

Relocated Pitot Tube

This BT-9 was assigned to the 91st Observation Squadron based at Fort Lewis, Washington. The rear portion of the cockpit canopy slid forward and down to act as a windscreen for the pilot in the rear seat when flying with the canopy open (which was a common practice). (AFM)

A BT-9A on the ramp at Randolph Field, Texas. Early BT-9As featured outer wing leading edge slats, which were ordered by the Army to counter the BT-9's unfavorable wingtip stall characteristics. This BT-9A carries a Flight Leader's stripe around the rear fuselage. (AFM)

9

The BT-9C was an improved version of the BT-9A with wing leading edge slats, a single .30 caliber machine gun mounted in the cowling, and a telescopic gun sight for the pilot. North American built thirty-two BT-9Cs specifically for the U.S. Army Organized Reserve. (Larkins)

This BT-9B (37-166) has had the fabric-covered fuselage panels replaced with all-metal panels from a BT-14. The poor fit of the panel joint line under the tail is a result of the length difference between the BT-9 and BT-14 which made it necessary to trim the panels. (Taylor)

The BT-9 was selected by the Navy to be its standard trainer under the designation NJ-1. The NJ-1 differed from the BT-9 in having a Navy-specified 500 hp Pratt & Whitney R-1340-6 Wasp engine, and a modified cowling with the exhaust exiting through two stacks under the cowl. (Starinchak)

Cowlings

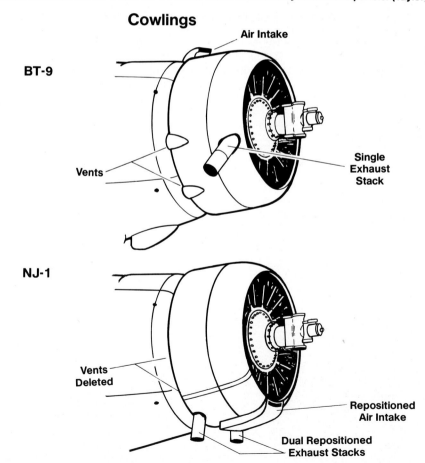

BT-9

Air Intake

Vents

Single Exhaust Stack

NJ-1

Vents Deleted

Repositioned Air Intake

Dual Repositioned Exhaust Stacks

BT-14/Yale Mk I

Based on their experience with the NJ-1, North American chose the 450 hp Pratt & Whitney R-985-25 Wasp Junior engine to power the next version of the BT-9, the BT-9D. The BT-9D, factory code NA-58, differed significantly from the earlier BT-9 variants. The fabric covered fuselage was replaced with a semi-monocoque all aluminum fuselage which was fourteen inches longer than the BT-9C. The shape of the vertical tail surfaces was changed with the leading edge being much more raked and the curved rudder was replaced by a more angular shaped rudder. The cowling was larger and the exhaust stack was repositioned to just behind the cowling midway up on the starboard fuselage. The wing was redesigned, being of a broader chord with squared off wingtips. These squared off tips reduced the wing span to forty-one feet. After inspecting the first aircraft, now re-designated the YBT-14, the Army ordered 251 aircraft under the designation BT-14. During 1941, twenty-seven BT-14s were modified to BT-14A standards by fitting them with the 400 hp Pratt & Whitney R-985-11A engine.

The Yale Mk I was essentially an export version of the BT-9B and BT-14. North American's first export customer was France, which ordered 230 aircraft under the company designation NA-57. The NA-57 was basically a BT-9B, with French equipment such as reversed throttles, and a 420 hp Wright R-975-E3 engine. All but sixteen aircraft had been delivered by the time the French fell to the Germans in June of 1940. The sixteen aircraft that had not been delivered were diverted to the Royal Canadian Air Force where they received the designation Yale Mk I. The French had also ordered 230 NA-64s, which were basically BT-14s with the Pratt & Whitney R-985-25 engines and reverse throttle arrangement. Deliveries of the French NA-64s had begun during late 1939, and once again those aircraft (119) not delivered before the fall of France were diverted to Canada where they too were designated as Yale Mk Is. A number of NA-57 and NA-64 aircraft that had been delivered to France fell into the hands of the Germans. These aircraft were put to use in the training role by the Vichy French Air Force and the Luftwaffe until at least 1942. The Yale Mk Is, even with their reverse throttles, served in RAF/RCAF training units in North America throughout the war years.

Student pilots of the 52nd School Squadron man their BT-14s on the ramp at Randolph Field, Texas during 1940. Randolph Field had 150 BT-14s assigned and was turning out 400 new Army pilots every five weeks. The seventy flight hour basic course took ten weeks to complete. (USAF)

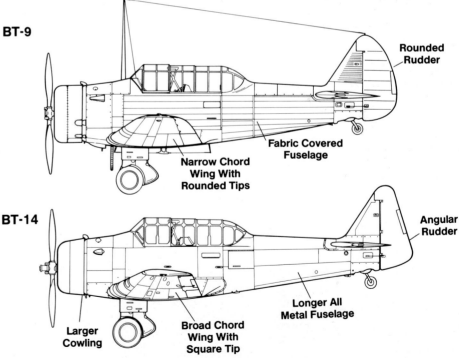

BT-9

Rounded Rudder

Narrow Chord Wing With Rounded Tips

Fabric Covered Fuselage

BT-14

Angular Rudder

Larger Cowling

Broad Chord Wing With Square Tip

Longer All Metal Fuselage

The BT-14 featured an all-metal fuselage that was fourteen inches longer than the BT-9, square wingtips, and a triangular shaped rudder. The BT-14 was powered by a 450 hp Wright R-985-27 Wasp Junior air cooled radial engine. (AFM)

BT-14s were also assigned to operational units for use as both a trainer and as a utility aircraft (hacks). This BT-14 of the 32nd Bomb Squadron/19th Bomb Group was based at Albuquerque, New Mexico during 1940. (Larkins)

This BT-14 of the 52nd School Squadron carries a full set of school identification markings on the upper left and lower right wing in Black. These markings were displayed prominently so that civilians could identify any low flying aircraft over a populated area. This practice led to the term — buzz number. (Taylor)

The French received a total of 214 NA-23s (BT-9Bs) before France fell to the Germans during 1940. The captured aircraft were later used by both the Luftwaffe and Vichy French Air Force. The NA-23s had been delivered from the factory in a camouflage of Brown and Green uppersurfaces over Light Gray undersurfaces. (Smithsonian)

This ex-French Air Force NA-64 (BT-14) was one of 111 received before France fell to the Nazis. Fifty of the NA-64s were captured and used by the Luftwaffe as trainers. Red 6 was assigned to the *Sonder Flugzeugfuhrer Schule* at Gottingen, and is painted overall Yellow with a Black anti-glare panel and markings. (AFM)

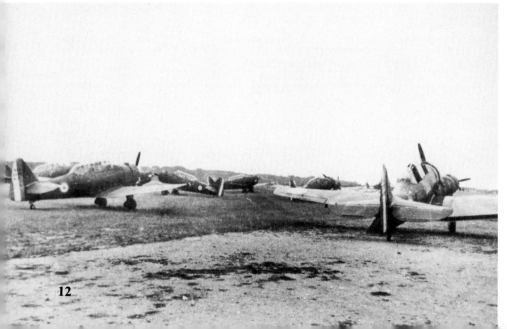

BC-1/SNJ-1 Series

When the design team at North American Aviation decided to modify the NA-16 series to incorporate fully retractable landing gear, it set the pattern for all the variants that followed. Whether the designation was BC-1, AT-6, SNJ, Harvard, or Wirraway, the airframe was basically the same. The mission of the NA-16 series and follow on variants was that of basic trainer/high performance fighter-trainer. North American was also successful in marketing variants of the NA-16 series to a number of nations as a general purpose aircraft that could be used in a number of roles.

North American also used the basic NA-16 technology to develop fighter and attack bomber variants. Later, this same basic aircraft would be modified to fill the forward air control and counter-insurgency roles. The retractable landing gear NA-16 series of aircraft set records for versatility and longevity that have yet to be matched.

BC-1

With the acceptance by both the Army and the Navy of NA-16 variants as their basic trainer aircraft, North American proposed several major changes intended to modernize the basic aircraft and improve its performance. Foremost among these proposals was a modification of the NA-16 to incorporate a fully retractable landing gear and an all metal fuselage. The latter change was proposed even before the first flight of the BT-14.

North American naturally intended this proposed improved trainer aircraft for both the U.S. Army and Navy hoping to sell the aircraft in quantity to the U.S. Government. At this time, the Army and Congress were only interested in buying combat type aircraft (fighters, bombers, etc.) and there was little money budgeted toward trainers. Dutch Kindelberger responded to the budget restriction by informing the Army Air Force commander, General Hap Arnold, that the new trainer design was actually a new class of combat aircraft, armed with .30 caliber machine guns and proposed that this new class of aircraft should be designated as a Basic Combat (BC) type. GEN Arnold liked the idea and announced a "competition" for a Basic Combat type. Since the "competition" was written around the North American design proposal, the company was an easy victor.

The prototype BC-1, company designation NA-36, although retaining the fabric covered fuselage of the BT-9, differed from the BT-9/BT-14 series in a number of ways: the landing gear was changed from fixed to fully retractable with the main wheels retracting into wells in the center section of the wing, the wing center section was increased in span by one foot to make room for the landing gear wheel wells, the outer wing panels were redesigned, the canopy was revised, and the aircraft was fitted with armament. The armament consisted of one .30 caliber machine gun mounted in the starboard side of the cowling and a second .30 caliber gun in the rear cockpit on a flexible mount.

The prototype BC-1 took to the air for the first time on 11 February 1938, one day after the first flight of the BT-14. Following flight tests with the prototype, the rudder was enlarged and flattened at the bottom to improve directional control. The BC-1 was powered by a 550 hp Pratt & Whitney R-1340-47 Wasp engine driving a two blade controllable pitch propeller. Although the BC-1 weighed over 5,100 pounds , the more powerful engine, along with the streamlining afforded by the retractable main landing gear, gave the BC-1 an additional 19 mph in top speed, from 190 mph to 209 mph.

Following a successful series of test flights, the Army ordered the aircraft into production under the designation BC-1. The initial Army contract called for the production of 180 aircraft; of these thirty-six were to be completed as instrument trainers under the designation BC-1I.

The North American NA-36 was the prototype for the BC-1 trainer series. It featured a fully retractable landing gear and was powered by a 600 hp Pratt and Whitney R-1340-S3H1 air cooled radial engine. The Army originally designated the prototype as the BT-9D. (AFM)

SNJ-1

During 1938 the Navy issued a requirement for a scout trainer to train pilots for the new high performance monoplane scout aircraft (such as the SBD) entering the Fleet. After evaluating the Air Corps BC-1, the Navy issued a detailed specification to North American for a new trainer under the designation SNJ-1 on 29 September 1938. The SNJ-1, factory code NA-52, was a combination of the best features of the basic BC-1, Navy specified changes, and North American updates.

The SNJ-1 blended the all-metal fuselage of the BT-14, the retractable landing gear wing of the BC-1 (with shortened outer wing panels and squared off wingtips), and the rounded flat-bottomed rudder used on production BC-1s. The Navy specified that the aircraft was to be powered by a 500 hp Pratt & Whitney R-1340-6 engine driving a two blade controllable pitch propeller instead of the 550 hp Pratt & Whitney R-1340-47. After a series of successful test flights the Navy ordered sixteen aircraft with the first SNJ-1 being delivered to NAS Anacostia on 29 May 1939.

This BC-1 of the 4th Air Base Squadron was based at March Field, California during 1938. The BC-1 retained the fabric-covered fuselage of the BT-9 series and was powered by the 500 hp Pratt & Whitney Wasp engine. (Larkins)

A pair of BC-1s from Randolph Field, Texas fly a practice formation flight during 1941. The distinctive ADF ring antenna just forward of the landing gear was a standard feature of BC-1 and BC-1A aircraft. Both aircraft carry Red cowlings with Yellow numbers. (AFM)

This BC-1 was assigned to the 3rd Air Base Squadron at Selfridge Field, Michigan. The distinctive shape of the NA-16 wing closely resembled that of a scaled down DC-2/3 airliner wing (which is understandable since its designers were ex-Douglas engineers). (AFM)

North American's plant at Inglewood, California was building BC-1 trainers and O-47A observation aircraft simultaneously. Between 1937 and 1940 North American built a total of 177 BC-1s and 239 O-47As. (AFM)

Landing Gear

BT-9/14

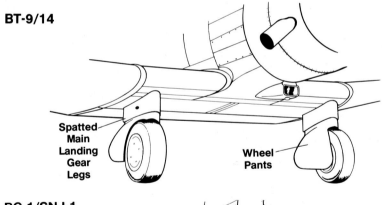

Spatted Main Landing Gear Legs

Wheel Pants

BC-1/SNJ-1

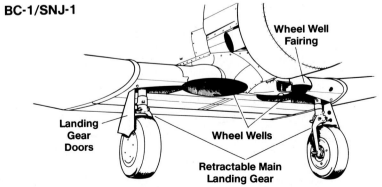

Wheel Well Fairing

Landing Gear Doors

Wheel Wells

Retractable Main Landing Gear

This BC-1 carries the Black and Yellow checkered cowling and wheel covers of the Army Command and Staff School and a school insignia on the rear fuselage. The loop between the landing gear is an ADF antenna. (Kemp via Menard)

The SNJ-1 was the first variant to combine the all-metal fuselage of the BT-14, retractable landing gear, and 500 hp Pratt & Whitney R-1340 Wasp engine. This SNJ-1 (BuNo 1552) was the first of sixteen SNJ-1s built for the Navy. (Larkins)

An SNJ-1 instrument trainer on a training mission during 1940. Navy trainer paint schemes were very colorful and consisted of a natural metal fuselage and wing undersurface, Yellow upper wing surfaces, Red cowling and tail, and a Black anti-glare panel. Instrument trainers carried a Red band around the fuselage and wings. (Starinchak)

Rudder

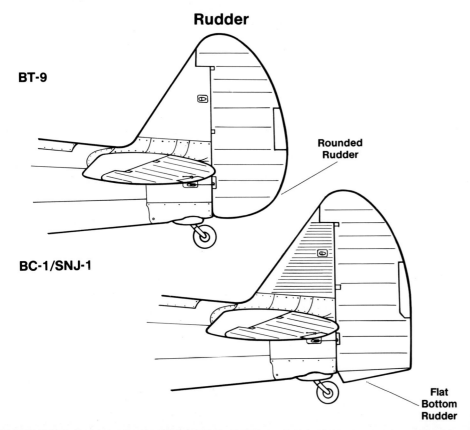

BT-9

Rounded Rudder

BC-1/SNJ-1

Flat Bottom Rudder

BC-1A (AT-6)

During the development of the BC series, there had been two features that the Army, Navy, and North American all wanted included in all future NA-16 variants — the all-metal fuselage and retractable landing gear wing. The all metal fuselage was the main difference between the BT-9 and BT-14. The retractable landing gear was incorporated into the BC-1 although it retained the fabric covered fuselage of the BT-9. In the SNJ-1, North American had combined the all metal fuselage of the BT-14 and retractable landing gear wing of the BC-1. After examining the SNJ-1 the Army decided to also adopt this combination and designated the new aircraft the BC-2.

The BC-2 incorporated the lengthened BT-14 semi-monocoque all-metal fuselage mated with the retractable landing gear BC-1 wing. The aircraft was powered by a 600 hp Pratt & Whitney R-1340-45 engine driving a three blade propeller. The air intake on the front underside of the cowling was repositioned to the underside of the fuselage just behind the cowling and a second large air intake was added midway up the port side of the fuselage just behind the cowling. The aircraft also featured the broader chord wing with squared off wingtips and angular shaped rudder of the BT-14.

Early flight tests with the prototype at Wright Field, Ohio, quickly revealed that the three bladed propeller did not increase performance enough to warrant its use on production aircraft and it was deleted from the trainer's specification. Production BC-1s were equipped with a two blade constant speed propeller.

Just before the aircraft went into production, the Army changed the designation from BC-2 to BC-1A (factory code NA-55). Initially the Army ordered eighty-three BC-1As, twenty-nine aircraft for delivery to the National Guard and fifty-four for the Army Reserve. These were followed by another nine aircraft which were ordered under a new designation. The Army had re-evaluated the Basic Combat category and had decided that these aircraft should be redesignated as Advanced Trainers. Under this policy change, the BC-1A became the AT-6 (factory code NA-59). The Army ordered another eighty-five aircraft under the AT-6 designation, most of these being assigned as gunnery trainers for air gunners. Total production of BC-1As/AT-6s was 177 aircraft.

The BC-1A combined the lengthened, all-metal fuselage of the BT-14 with a triangular rudder, and a widened BC-1 retractable landing gear wing which was modified with squared off wingtips similar to those on the BT-14. (Besecker via Dorr)

This highly polished BC-1A (39-849) was assigned to a California Air Corps Reserve unit based at Long Beach during 1940. The rear canopy folded forward in the stowed position and acted as a windscreen for the crewman in the rear seat. (Larkins)

Fuselage Development

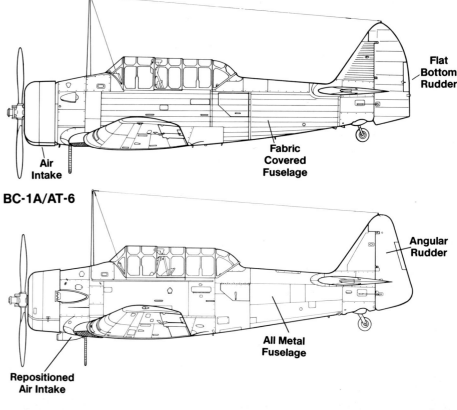

BC-1

Flat Bottom Rudder

Air Intake

Fabric Covered Fuselage

BC-1A/AT-6

Angular Rudder

All Metal Fuselage

Repositioned Air Intake

Flying cadet Boardman C. Reed solos in an AT-6 over Kelly Field, Texas during 1940. The BC-1A became the AT-6 when the Army Air Corps changed the aircraft's mission code from Basic Combat to Advanced Trainer. The cowling is in Yellow with Black numbers.

This AT-6 was assigned to the 79th Pursuit Squadron/20th Pursuit Group based at Hamilton Field, California during 1941. AT-6s assigned to combat units often carried the colors and markings of the unit's primary aircraft. (Larkins)

Wing Development

BC-1/SNJ-1

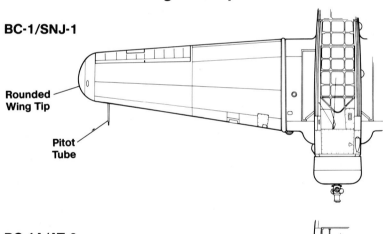

Rounded
Wing Tip

Pitot
Tube

BC-1A/AT-6

Squared
Off
Wing Tip

Relocated
Pitot Tube

Womans Air Service Pilots (WASPs) also trained in the AT-6. A large part of the WASPs mission was ferrying the modern Army and Navy aircraft to bases both in the US and overseas. This group of WASP cadets is planning a cross-country flight out of Avenger Field, Texas. (AFM)

Attack and Fighter Variants

NA-44/A-27

Two armed variants of the NA-16 were built by North American specifically for the export market; one was a two seat fighter/attack aircraft and the other was a single seat fighter. The two seat fighter/attack aircraft was given the company designation NA-44 and was originally built for the Siamese (Thai) Air Force. The aircraft was basically a BC-1A re-engined with a 785 hp Wright R-1820-F52 Cyclone engine driving a three bladed propeller. The NA-44 was armed with five .30 caliber machine guns; two mounted in the cowling, one in each wing, and another on a flexible mount in the rear cockpit. Underwing bomb racks were fitted which were capable of carrying up to 400 pounds of bombs, along with a centerline bomb rack capable of carying a 500 pound bomb.

The NA-44 was a success on the export market, with at least fifty-two aircraft being sold to three countries. Siam (Thailand) bought ten aircraft under the company designation NA-69 (the North American company numbers changed for each export customer), Brazil purchased thirty NA-72s, and Chile ordered twelve NA-74s. During the Summer of 1940, increasing political tension between French Indochina and Siam led the U.S. State Department to revoke North American's export permits for the NA-69 while the aircraft were in the Philippines awaiting further shipment to Thailand. The aircraft were taken over by the U.S. Army Air Corps, receiving the U.S. Army designation A-27. The aircraft were turned over to the USAAC fighter squadrons in the Philippines for use as trainers and were on hand when the Japanese attacked the Philippines on 8 December 1941. Although all of the A-27s were put out of action that first day, several were put back into flyable condition and flew scouting and bombing missions during the next few weeks before they were finally destroyed in action.

NA-50A/NA-68/P-64

The single seat fighter developed from the NA-16 was originally designed to meet Siamese (Thai) Air Force specifications. The aircraft, designated the NA-50A, was powered by an 870 hp Wright R-1820-77 engine driving a three blade propeller. The wingspan of the NA-50A was some five feet shorter than the AT-6. It was armed with two .30 caliber Colt-Browning machine guns mounted in the cowling, one in each wing, and it had provision for bomb racks beneath the wings for up to 550 pounds of bombs. The fuselage, one foot shorter than the AT-6, was completely redesigned from the windscreen back, with a shorter canopy and sloping turtleback fuselage. The aircraft had the same fin and rudder as the BC-1.

The prototype, company designation NA-50A, flew for the first time on 1 September 1940. Flight tests showed a speed of 295 mph, a range of 645 miles, and a service ceiling of 32,000 feet. Peru bought seven aircraft under the designation NA-50A, all of which were delivered during the Spring of 1939. These aircraft saw combat during a brief border war between Peru and Ecuador during 1941. During the fighting, one NA-50A was shot down by ground fire, the only NA-50A lost in combat.

Siam (Thailand) tested the NA-50A during September of 1939 and ordered six modified NA-50 aircraft under the designation NA-68. The NA-68 differed from the NA-50A in having the angular AT-6 style rudder, improved landing gear doors, and revised armament. The NA-68 carried a single 20mm cannon mounted in a gondola under each wing along with four 8mm machine guns two in the cowling and two in the wings. The aircraft destined for Siam were aboard ship in Hawaii when the State Department (as with the NA-69s) revoked the export permits. The aircraft were shipped back to California, stripped of their armament, and taken over by the U.S. Army Air Corps for use as fighter-

Two of the ten NA-69 attack aircraft built for Siam (armed BC-1As) on the ramp at Nichols Field in the Philippines during late 1941. The NA-69s were repossessed by the Army, redesignated as A-27s, and flew combat missions against the Japanese after the 8 December 1941 attack on American bases in the Philippines. (AFM)

trainers at Luke Army Air Base under the designation P-64. Throughout their career in the Training Command the P-64s retained their Thai camouflage finish of Dark Brown and Dark Green uppersurfaces over Light Gray undersurfaces. After the war, five of the P-64s were scrapped. The lone surviving P-64 was later sold to a civilian who restored the aircraft in a pre-Second World War type paint scheme. The aircraft was later purchased by the Experimental Aircraft Association based in Oshkosh, Wisconsin.

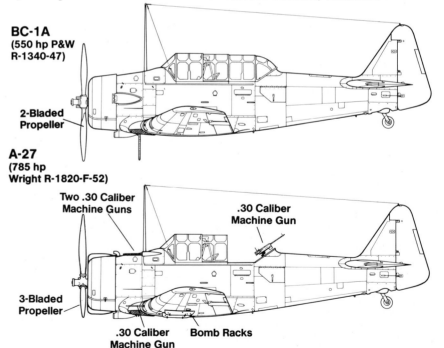

BC-1A
(550 hp P&W R-1340-47)

2-Bladed Propeller

A-27
(785 hp Wright R-1820-F-52)

Two .30 Caliber Machine Guns

.30 Caliber Machine Gun

3-Bladed Propeller

.30 Caliber Machine Gun

Bomb Racks

Fighter Variants

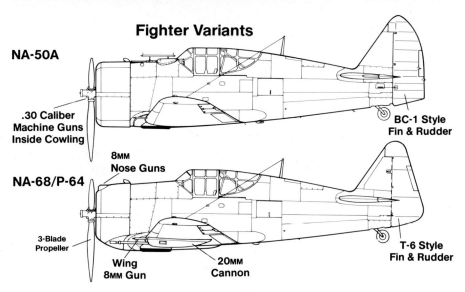

NA-50A

.30 Caliber
Machine Guns
Inside Cowling

BC-1 Style
Fin & Rudder

NA-68/P-64

8MM
Nose Guns

3-Blade
Propeller

Wing
8MM Gun

20MM
Cannon

T-6 Style
Fin & Rudder

(Below) The NA-68 (P-64) was a single seat fighter developed from the AT-6. The fuselage was one foot shorter than an AT-6 and the wings were reduced by five feet. Powered by an 870 hp engine, the P-64 had a top speed of 295 mph. Six were built for Siam but were never delivered. The Siamese aircraft were taken over by the Army during 1941 and used as fighter-trainers. (Bamberger)

(Above) One of the seven NA-50A fighters built by North American for export to Peru. These aircraft saw combat during 1941 when Peru and Ecuador fought a border war. One of the NA-50As was shot down by ground fire and it is believed that this was the only Peruvian Air Force loss during the entire war. (NAA)

19

SNJ-2

The SNJ-2 (NA-65) was basically a refinement of the earlier SNJ-1. The oil cooler was moved to the port side of the engine making it necessary to install a small vent scoop behind the cowling on the port side. The carburetor air intake scoop was moved from under the cowl to a position on the port side of the fuselage immediately behind the cowling. The cowl ring was enlarged, becoming broader in chord.

The rounded rudder of the SNJ-1 was retained, as were the Navy requirements for a pilots chart board and leather headrest. The aircraft was powered by a Navy specified 600 hp Pratt & Whitney R-1340-36 driving a two blade propeller. The SNJ-2 made its first flight on 29 March 1940 with deliveries to Navy units beginning in May of that same year. The Navy was pleased with the SNJ-2 which demonstrated a top speed of 214 mph, a service ceiling in excess of 24,000 feet, and a rate of climb of 1,200 feet per minute. The majority of the aircraft in the first production contract (thirty-six aircraft) were delivered to Naval Reserve units. As Navy training requirements changed, a new contract for SNJ-2s was issued for an additional twenty-five aircraft, for a total production run of sixty-one SNJ-2s.

RADM Aubrey Fitch was Commander of Carrier Division One during 1941 and had this SNJ-2 assigned as his personal aircraft. The fuselage was in Command Blue, the tail was White, the fuselage lettering was Yellow, and the wings had Chrome Yellow uppersurfaces with natural metal undersurfaces. A metal frame has been installed under the front cockpit to hold the Admiral's two star placard. (Bowers via Larkins)

An SNJ-2 of the Naval Reserve Aviation Base (NRAB), New York. The SNJ-2 retained the rounded rudder of the BC-1/SNJ-1 and had the antenna mast mounted centrally in front of the windscreen. This aircraft is painted in the standard Navy trainer scheme with the cowling, tail, and fuselage band in True Blue. (Larkins)

An SNJ-2 of the Oakland, California Naval Air Reserve unit sits on the Oakland ramp next to a Grumman Duck on 7 December 1941. Later that day the base initiated very tight security procedures that forbade cameras on the base and ramp. (Larkins)

AT-6A/B, SNJ-3

With the introduction of the AT-6A/SNJ-3 variants, the Army and Navy finally standardized most of the features on the North Amercan trainer. T-6A/SNJ-3s became almost totally interchangable aircraft and were externally idential. Army contract AC-15977 and Navy BuAer Requisition 1255 both specified the same basic airframe, wing, vertical fin, and engine (with minor moifications), with the Navy accepting the triangular vertical fin and rudder of the T-6 for the SNJ-3.

The instrument panels were redesigned and the rear canopy was modified so that it could be folded forward to serve as a windscreen for the rear crewman. Navy aircraft were powered by a 600 hp Pratt & Whitney R-1340-AN-1 engine, while Army aircraft were fitted with a 600 hp Pratt & Whitney R-1340-49 engine (these engines were virtually identical except for minor equipment changes that the Navy required). Both the SNJ-3 (NA-78) and AT-6A (NA-77) could be armed with a single .30 caliber machine gun in the upper starboard cowling and a flexible .30 caliber gun in the rear cockpit. For gunnery training, the rear cockpit was fitted with a 360° fully swiveling seat. The SNJ-3C, and all subsequent SNJs given the C suffix, was a standard SNJ-3 fitted with a tail hook under the rear fuselage for carrier qualification training. A total of fifty-five SNJ-3s were modified to SNJ-3C standards at NAS Pensacola.

So close was the commonality between the two aircraft that the Army actually accepted the first SNJ-3 for the Navy. The first flight of an SNJ-3 took place during early March of 1941. Deliveries to NAS Anacostia began that same month. With an Army contract for 517 AT-6As, a Navy contract for 120 SNJ-3s, plus an RAF contract for 526 Harvard IIs (BC-1As), North American found its production line was once again becoming overloaded.

Faced with a need to expand production, Kindelberger decided to build a second North American plant in Dallas, Texas. This plant would be devoted to building T-6/SNJ trainers. Aircraft built at the Inglewood plant (NA-77s) would carry the suffix NA; while those built in the Dallas plant (NA-78s) were suffixed NT. The Dallas plant would be the prime contractor for the T-6 series from this point forward, with an almost 7-1 ratio of finished airframes over the California plant.

This is where the aircraft's name TEXAN originated — from the fact that the majority of the series were built in Texas. Perhaps it was also a coincidence that a large number of Army and Navy training airfields were also in Texas, simply adding to the growing Texan legend.

With the introduction of the AT-6B, Army and Navy production aircraft became even more identical. The main difference between the Army AT-6A and Navy SNJ-3 had been in the engine used. With the AT-6B (NA-84), the Army changed engines also adopting the R-1340-AN-1 engine. The AT-6B also incorporated additional armament in the form of a .30 caliber machine gun mounted in the starboard wing and underwing bomb racks for up to four 100 pound bombs. Additionally the rear seat was permanently mounted facing rearward since AT-6Bs were intended to be primarily gunnery trainers. A total of 1,400 AT-6Bs were built at the Dallas plant.

A flight of AT-6As over Kelly Field, Texas during 1941. These AT-6As are fitted with target-tow cable mounts under the aft fuselage for towing gunnery targets. The cowling color of 305, 308, and 315 is White, while 700 and 703 have Red cowlings. (AFM)

Rudder

SNJ-2

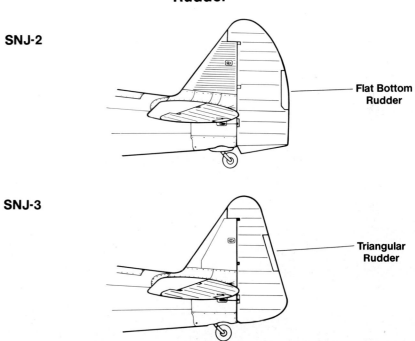

— Flat Bottom Rudder

SNJ-3

— Triangular Rudder

This AT-6A stationed at Stockton Field, California is mounted on jacks for use as an AT-6 cockpit orientation trainer. It was not unusual for a new cadet to pull the wrong handle and fold up the landing gear while sitting on the ramp. By using the cockpit orientation trainer, these incidents were reduced. (Dorr)

A pair of AT-6As from Mather Field (coded T) parked on the dirt at Moffet Field in March of 1942. The large hanger in the background was built for the lighter-than-air ship, USS Macon. The AT-6A in the foreground is unusual in that it has the serial number on the fuselage instead of the vertical tail. The AT-6A behind T-138 is in the trainer scheme of Blue with Yellow wings. (Larkins)

A flight of three Red nosed AT-6As fly formation over Kelly Field during 1943. By 1943 the Red, White, and Blue rudder stripes had been removed from US aircraft, including trainers. These aircraft are not equipped with a pilot's headrest which was normally installed on Army AT-6s. (Taylor)

After the war many AT-6s were sold as surplus. Western Airlines purchased two AT-6As and an AT-6C for flying mail on the airline's routes in the Dakotas. This AT-6A, registered NC 63082, carried the same Western Airlines markings as the company's larger airliners. (WAL via Dorr)

This SNJ-3 was assigned to the Naval Air Station at Alameda, California during 1940. The SNJ-3 was virtually identical to the AT-6A, and was the first T-6 variant to be powered by an -AN engine. The -AN designation meant that the engine was accepted as standard for both Army and Navy use. (Taylor)

Armament

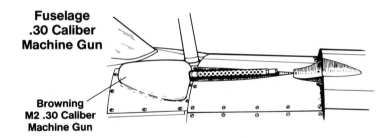

Fuselage
.30 Caliber
Machine Gun

Browning
M2 .30 Caliber
Machine Gun

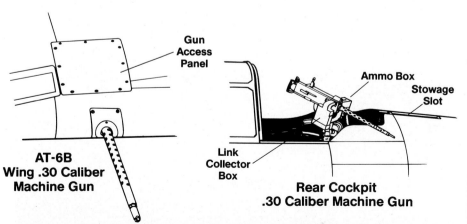

Gun
Access
Panel

AT-6B
Wing .30 Caliber
Machine Gun

Ammo Box

Stowage
Slot

Link
Collector
Box

Rear Cockpit
.30 Caliber Machine Gun

An SNJ-3 and SBC-4 Helldiver of the First Marine Aircraft Wing fly together near Quantico, Virginia. Both aircraft are camouflaged with Intermediate Blue Gray uppersurfaces over Light Gray undersurfaces. The SNJ-3 was used as a gunnery trainer, while the SBC-4 was used in the dive bomber training role. (Starinchak)

This SNJ-3 on the ramp at NAS Moffet Field, California during 1944 was used as a station hack/utility aircraft. Utility aircraft rated a low maintenance and repainting priority and this SNJ shows it. The three tone camouflage scheme has faded badly. The port wing has been completely repainted while the starboard wing has not. (Starinchak)

AT-6C/SNJ-4

The AT-6C/SNJ-4 (both coded NA-88) were externally identical to the earlier AT-6B although featuring a number of internal changes. The SNJ-4 was the first of the SNJ series to have provision for the wing mounted .30 caliber machine gun and underwing bomb racks. Deliveries of AT-6Cs and SNJ-4s began in June of 1942. With production of the AT-6C/SNJ-4 well underway, the War Department began having grave misgivings over the impact of German U-boats on aluminum imports. If the U-boats could not be stopped, a severe shortage of aluminum was highly likely. A substantial amount of aluminum was being expended in the manufacture of trainer aircraft and the War Department felt that this same aluminum would be put to better use building offensive and defensive combat aircraft.

With this in mind, the War Department issued directives that requested all American aircraft manufacturers to try and find substitutes for aluminum wherever possible. North American answered this request by designing and building a number of wooden parts for the AT-6C/SNJ-4. Initially the horizontal stabilizers, control columns, and various floor portions were made of wood. Then, beginning with the AT-6C-10, the entire rear fuselage skinning and bulkheads were changed to molded three-ply mahogany plywood, while the fuselage internal stringers, stiffeners, bulkhead flanges and longerons were changed from aluminum to solid spruce.

The wooden AT-6C/SNJ-4s were extremely strong, although their durability suffered when exposed to humid climates for long periods. While the wooden Texans were actually somewhat heavier than the all-metal versions, pilots often reported that they felt lighter on the controls.

Through the use of molded plywood, some 200 pounds of aluminum were saved on each T-6 built. During the AT-6C production run, a total of 2,222 were built. Of these, 1,243 had plywood fuselages. Of the 2,401 SNJ-4s built, 1,040 had plywood rear fuselages. Over the course of the AT-6C/SNJ-4 production run, a total of 420,000 pounds of aluminum was saved for use on fighters and bombers.

Eighty-five of the all-metal SNJ-4s were modified with tail hooks for carrier operations and redesignated SNJ-4Cs.

AT-6D/SNJ-5

The AT-6D and SNJ-5 (both coded NA-88), were follow on programs from the earlier AT-6C/SNJ-4 and were virtually identical with the exception of the electrical systems. In all previous Texan variants the electrical system was a 12 volt system. The AT-6D/SNJ-5 had a 24 volt system installed.

Since the AT-6D/SNJ-5s were coming off the Dallas assembly line intermixed with AT-6C/SNJ-4s, a number of these airframes were built with wooden rear assemblies, although the majority of AT-6D/SNJ-4s reverted to the all-metal construction.

A grand total of 3,958 AT-6Ds (440 with wood assemblies) were built along with a total of 2,198 SNJ-5s (276 with wood assemblies). Eighty SNJ-5s were fitted with tail hooks and redesignated SNJ-5Cs. Deliveries of this series began during the Summer of 1943.

A flight of AT-6Cs based at Randolph Field during 1943 fly a practice formation flight. North American built 443 AT-6C-10s which had a molded plywood rear fuselage. These aircraft sections were painted Aluminum dope. Another 160 AT-6Cs were produced with plywood cockpit flooring and horizontal tail surfaces. (AFM)

A student gunner takes aim from the rear cockpit of an AT-6C gunnery trainer based at Fort Myers (base code FM), Florida, during 1942. Bomber gunners trained in the rear cockpit of AT-6s before graduating to bombers. The slot in the upper rear fuselage was used to store the .30 caliber machine gun when not in use. (Larkins)

A pair of AT-6Cs based at Luke Field fly over the country-side near Phoenix during 1943. By this date all North American T-6/SNJ/Harvard production was being carried out at its Dallas, Texas plant. These Texans have Gloss Dark Green cowlings. (USAF)

An SNJ-4 shoots a landing at Concord OLF (Outlying Field) near Naval Air Station Alameda, California during October of 1943. OLFs were used for practice takeoffs and landings. The SNJ has Intermediate Blue upper surfaces over Light Gray under surfaces with a Yellow R-7 on the fuselage overlapping the Red bordered national insignia. (Larkins)

Rear Fuselage Development

A Navy photographer readies his camera in the rear cockpit of an SNJ-4 of Carrier Air Service Unit (CASU) - 23. Most aircraft carriers had at least one SNJ assigned for use as a hack aircraft while in port. This SNJ has a Red fuselage band identifying it as an instrument trainer. (Dorr)

AT-6C/SNJ-4 (Early)

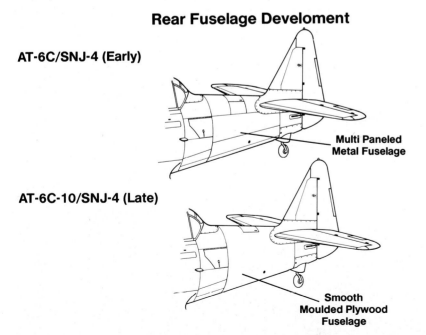

Multi Paneled Metal Fuselage

AT-6C-10/SNJ-4 (Late)

Smooth Moulded Plywood Fuselage

155239

The front instrument panel of an AT-6C Texan. The placard on the right corner of the panel reads: "Service this airplane with 91 octane fuel only, if not available, next higher grade will be used in an emergency." (AFM)

The instrument panel installed in the rear cockpit of the AT-6C. The cockpit color of the AT-6 was Interior Green with Black instrument panels, controls and radios. (AFM)

An SNJ-4 of the Oakland Naval Air Reserve unit flies over Oakland Bay during March of 1950. SNJs all carried code letters that identified their home base and F was the assigned code for Oakland. This Texan was overall natural metal with an Orange Reserve fuselage band. (Larkins)

This Red cowled AT-6D carries some unusual special markings. The words "Enlist In The AAF" were carried on Army Air Force aircraft during 1946 when enlistments were low. The letter B following the buzz number indicated that the aircraft was the second one in the unit to be assigned that number.

A quartet of T-6Ds assigned to Randolph AFB rest on jacks in preparation for cockpit orientation tests. When Congress created the U.S. Air Force during 1947, the Air Force immediately changed all the former Army Air Force designations, dropping the Advanced from AT-6 changing the designation to simply T-6D. (Ed Galbraith via Menard)

A T-6D instrument trainer of the California Air National Guard flies over San Francisco during October of 1949. Instrument trainers had canvas hoods that completely covered the pilot that was taking the instrument course. The aircraft is overall natural metal with the cowling, vertical tail, wingtips, and instrument trainer wing bands in Red. (Larkins)

An AT-6D of the European Air Transport Service on the ramp at Berlin's Tempelhof Airport during 1946. The AT-6D was externally identical to the AT-6C, the main difference being the electrical system. The AT-6C had a 12 volt system while the T-6D had a 24 volt system. The cowling and rudder of this Texan is in Medium Blue. (AFM)

One of the most colorful T-6Ds in the Air Force was assigned to the All-Weather Flying Center at Clinton County Air Force Base near Dayton, Ohio during 1947. The Red and Yellow striped Texan flew weather research missions into thunderstorms along side P-61C Black Widows from the same base. (Larkins)

A "CAPTIVAIR" T-6D at Perrin Air Force Base. The "CAPTIVAIR" system allowed a cadet to literally "fly' the aircraft, getting a feel for everything in the cockpit, without actually leaving the ground. The enlarged cowling and cooling fan kept the engine from overheating during ground runups. (Merritt via Menard)

During the immediate post-war years a number of National Guard units painted their state seal on the aircraft in place of the National insignia. This Nebraska National Guard T-6D was assigned to the 173rd FS. The last two digits of the aircraft number on the landing gear door has been reversed. (Balogh)

This SNJ-4 assigned to NAS Oakland, California is painted in the post-war Navy trainer scheme of overall Silver paint with an Orange reserve fuselage band. Interestingly, the hanger still retains its wartime camouflage even though the war has been over for several years. (Larkins)

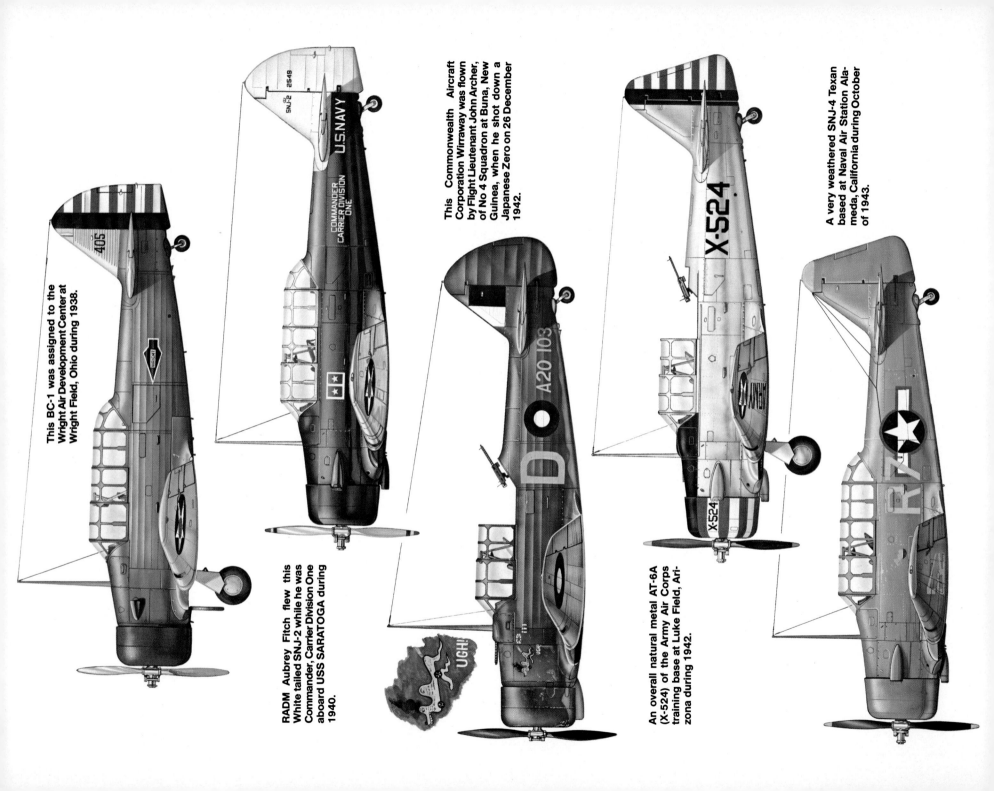

This BC-1 was assigned to the Wright Air Development Center at Wright Field, Ohio during 1938.

RADM Aubrey Fitch flew this White tailed SNJ-2 while he was Commander, Carrier Division One aboard USS SARATOGA during 1940.

This Commonwealth Aircraft Corporation Wirraway was flown by Flight Lieutenant John Archer, of No 4 Squadron at Buna, New Guinea, when he shot down a Japanese Zero on 26 December 1942.

An overall natural metal AT-6A (X-524) of the Army Air Corps training base at Luke Field, Arizona during 1942.

A very weathered SNJ-4 Texan based at Naval Air Station Alameda, California during October of 1943.

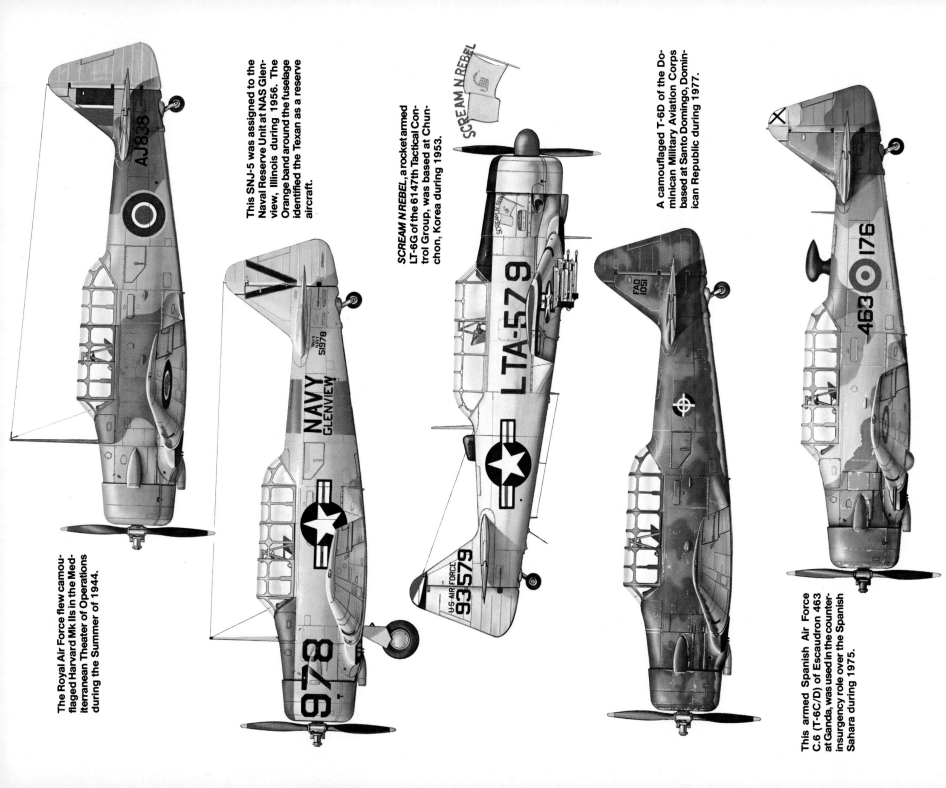

The Royal Air Force flew camouflaged Harvard Mk IIs in the Mediterranean Theater of Operations during the Summer of 1944.

This SNJ-5 was assigned to the Naval Reserve Unit at NAS Glenview, Illinois during 1956. The Orange band around the fuselage identified the Texan as a reserve aircraft.

SCREAM N REBEL, a rocket armed LT-6G of the 6147th Tactical Control Group, was based at Chunchon, Korea during 1953.

A camouflaged T-6D of the Dominican Military Aviation Corps based at Santo Domingo, Dominican Republic during 1977.

This armed Spanish Air Force C.6 (T-6C/D) of Escaudron 463 at Ganda, was used in the counterinsurgency role over the Spanish Sahara during 1975.

An SNJ-5 flies lead for a pair of SNJ-4s of CASU-23. SNJ-4s and -5s were identical except for their electrical systems and they often served together in the same units. The large Green bands on the wings and fuselage indicate that the Texans are used as instrument trainers. (Larkins)

The flight deck officer gives the launch signal to the pilot of this SNJ-5C aboard USS WASP. Carriers had SNJs assigned as hacks/utility aircraft; however, they did not usually take them on deployment. The suffix C in the Texan's designation indicated that it was a tail hook equipped SNJ. (Larkins)

Arrestor Hook

SNJ-4

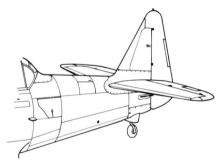

This SNJ pilot on final approach to USS WRIGHT during 1948 has the hook down to catch the carrier's arresting wire. Arrested landings were required as part of his Carrier Qualification. This SNJ has had the landing gear doors removed since they were often lost during carrier landings. (Ron Gerdes via Larkins)

SNJ-4C

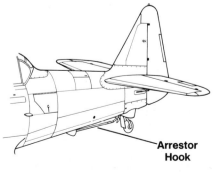

Arrestor Hook

A pair of SNJ-5s parked on the ramp at NAS Glenview during 1956. Each naval air station was assigned a code letter which was painted on the vertical tail, upper starboard and lower port wings. Additionally, all Reserve units had International Orange bands around the rear fuselage. (Menard)

This SNJ-5 at NAS Willow Grove carries the Reserve marking applied to SNJs near the end of their service careers. The 7 on the tail indicated a land-based unit, the W stood for Willow Grove, and the Orange fuselage band indicated reserve status. The aircraft also carries the newly adopted Red and White rescue markings on the fuselage. (Dorr)

These SNJ-5s have been lowered onto stacks of tires, then lashed down to the ramp in preparation for a hurricane or tropical storm at NAS Corry Field, Florida. A crane would hoist the aircraft up while a mechanic retracted the landing gear, then the aircraft was lowered onto the tires and lashed down. (John Kirk)

Although now privately owned, this SNJ-5 Texan previously served with the Spanish Air Force. Spain obtained a number of T-6s, SNJs, and various mark Harvards after the war, designating them (regardless of source) as C.6s. (Taylor)

XAT-6E

During 1944, the Army ordered an experimental variant of the AT-6D to test the feasibility of mounting an inline, air-cooled engine in the AT-6 airframe. This experiment was conducted for two reasons; most Army fighters of the period were powered by inline engines (P-40, P-39 and P-51s) and there existed a possibility that there could be a shortage of Pratt & Whitney Wasp engines since the demand for these engines was exceeding their output. The Army designated this experimental aircraft as the XAT-6E (the only Texan variant to carry an X designation).

One AT-6D airframe (42-84241) was modified with the 575 hp Ranger V-770-9, inverted V, twelve cylinder air-cooled high altitude engine driving a two blade propeller fitted with a spinner. Although only half as large in displacement as the Pratt & Whitney radial engine, the improvement in streamlining allowed by the slim lines of the inline engine made the XAT-6E the fastest of the T-6 series. The installation of the inline engine gave the XAT-6E a much longer nose section and led to a compete rebalancing of the aircraft. During flight tests at Eglin Army Air Force Base in Florida, the XAT-6E revealed a top speed of 244 mph and a service ceiling of 30,000 feet, some 6,000 feet higher than any of the radial engine T-6 variants.

The big Ranger engine, however, proved to be mechanically unreliable and a maintenance nightmare. Since the shortage of Wasp engines never materialized, the XAT-6E project never progressed beyond the prototype stage. The prototype XAT-6E survived the war and was later sold as surplus.

There have been reports of two XAT-6Es involved in civil air races after the war. North American records indicate only one XAT-6E was built and it is believed that this second aircraft was probably a private conversion of a surplus T-6 airframe. The North Amercan built aircraft was known to have been flown by its owner in several races during the late 1940s with the civil registration NX7410.

The XAT-6E was a standard AT-6D (42-84241), modified to mount a 575 hp Ranger V-770-9 twelve cylinder inline air-cooled engine. Technical problems with the engine led to the project being cancelled even though the XAT-6E proved to be the fastest T-6 variant. (AFM)

AT-6D

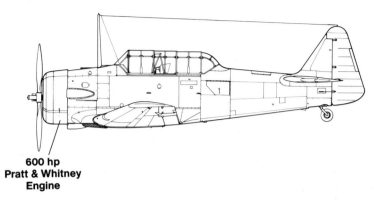

**600 hp
Pratt & Whitney
Engine**

XAT-6E

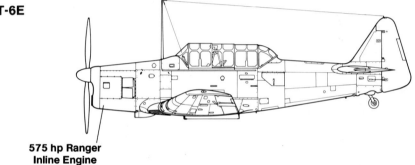

**575 hp Ranger
Inline Engine**

AT-6F/SNJ-6

The AT-6F/SNJ-6 (NA-121) was the last production variant of the T-6/SNJ series. These aircraft differed from the AT-6D/SNJ-5 in several ways. The rear cockpit armament was deleted completely and the swivelable rear seat was changed to a fixed forward facing seat. The rear cockpit compartment canopy was changed with a one-piece, non-moveable clear bubble canopy being installed in place of the movable rear canopy section of the AT-6D. The nose and wing-mounted guns were also removed, along with the underwing bomb racks. AT-6Fs were also fitted with a propeller spinner; however, these were often removed in the field by maintenance crews since the spinners made maintenance of the propeller hub and engine more difficult.

The AT-6F/SNJ-6 was the first Texan variant with provisions for carrying external fuel. A twenty gallon drop tank was mounted on a fuselage centerline rack just aft of the main wheel wells.

The Army contracted for a total of 1,375 aircraft; however, with the end of the war 417 of these were cancelled. North American built a total of 958 AT-6F/SNJ-6s. Of the airframes completed, 411 were delivered to the Navy as SNJ-6s.

None of the SNJ-6s are known to have been fitted with tail hooks.

Combat units usually had an AT-6 assigned for use as a hack/utility aircraft. These Texans carried VIPs and press people on base tours, as well as the unit commanders to their meetings. *Anita Theresa*, an AT-6F (44-81723) of the 364th FS/357th FG, carried the Group's Red and Yellow checked nose and a Yellow rudder. (Olmsted)

Propeller Spinner

T-6D

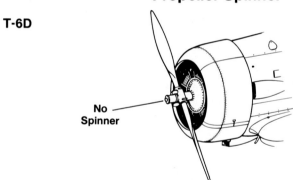

No Spinner

T-6F

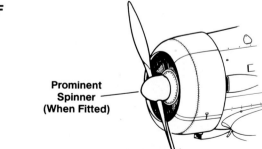

Prominent Spinner (When Fitted)

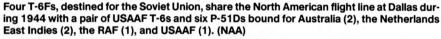

Four T-6Fs, destined for the Soviet Union, share the North American flight line at Dallas during 1944 with a pair of USAAF T-6s and six P-51Ds bound for Australia (2), the Netherlands East Indies (2), the RAF (1), and USAAF (1). (NAA)

This colorful T-6F Texan was assigned to the 36th FBG at Furstenfeldbruck, Germany during 1951. Support aircraft, like this T-6F, were often painted in unit colors. The Texan has a Blue and White tail and horizontal stabilizers — the same markings applied to the unit's F-84G Thunderjets. (Leo Kelley via Menard)

This highly polished SNJ-6 was the Commander's aircraft at Naval Air Station Alameda during 1947. The SNJ-6 was the Navy designation for the AT-6F. The propeller spinner and antiglare panel are gloss Dark Blue with Gold and Dark Blue striping. (Larkins)

Canopy Development

AT-6D

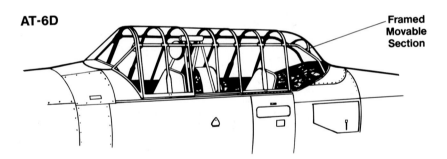

Framed
Movable
Section

This AT-6F, at Ladd Field, Alaska, is being inspected by Soviet ferry pilots before being dispatched to Siberia. These Texans were delivered to Ladd Field by members of the 7th Ferry Squadron. (Jeff Ethell via Stapfer)

AT-6F

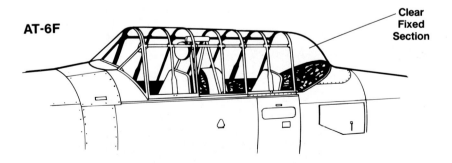

Clear
Fixed
Section

35

This well maintained T-6F was used at Wright Field to test several styles of centerline drop tanks. A twenty gallon tank was later adopted as a standard piece of equipment on the T-6G/LT-6G. This drop tank is an experimental fifty-five gallon tank. (Larkins)

An AT-6F buzzes the ramp at Coreopolis Army Air Force Base during 1946. The AT-6F was the first variant to have provisions for carrying a belly tank and usually carried a twenty gallon tank on the fuselage centerline. (Balogh via Menard)

Belly Tank Installation

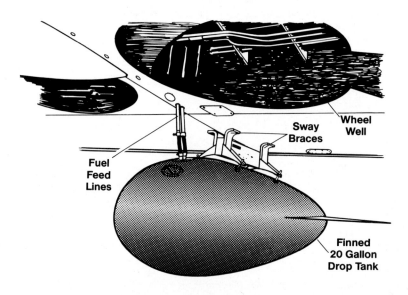

Wheel Well

Sway Braces

Fuel Feed Lines

Finned 20 Gallon Drop Tank

An overall Yellow SNJ-6 assigned to the Naval Air Reserve unit at Grosse Ile on the ramp at Detroit Airport during 1955. At this time the modex number on the nose repeated the last three digits of the aircraft's Bureau Number (BuNo). (Menard)

An AT-6F instrument trainer of an unidentified stateside training unit carries a Red nose and fuselage band. AT-6Fs not used for gunnery training normally had all the aircraft's armament and ordnance capabilities removed. (Balogh)

T-6s and SNJs of all variants were sold to other nations under the Mutual Defense Assistance Program (MDAP). This T-6F (ex-USAF 44-82500) went to Japan to train pilots for the Japanese Air Self Defense Force at Misawa AB during 1962. (Menard)

37

T-6G/SNJ-7

The final major variant of the T-6 family, the T-6G, was actually a remanufactured aircraft built from earlier T-6/SNJ airframes (the A prefix had been dropped from the Texan's designation during 1947 when the U.S. Air Force redesignated all trainer aircraft, both basic and advanced, as simply T). Four North American plants were involved in the conversion program; North American Downey, California; North American Fresno, California; Douglas Aircraft at Long Beach, California; and the newly purchased ex-Curtiss plant at Columbus, Ohio.

During the remanufacturing process, several modifications were made to the airframes to bring them up to T-6G (NA-168) standards. These included raising the rear seat six inches, addition of a P-51 Mustang steerable/lockable tail wheel system, elimination of several of the canopy metal frames for better visibility from the cockpit, updated radios, hydraulic systems changes, all provisions for internal machine guns were eliminated, and the aircraft were fitted with fifteen gallon bladder type fuel tanks in the outer wing panels. Finally, the rebuilt T-6Gs were painted overall trainer Yellow.

All the aircraft bore entirely new Air Force serial numbers with suffix letters indicating where they had completed the remanufacturing program; NI for Downey, NH for Columbus, NA for Long Beach, and NF for Fresno. It is interesting to note that when the Air Force decided to start the T-6G rebuild program there were not enough T-6 airframes in the Air Force inventory to fill the contract. With the end of the war, large number of T-6/SNJs had been sold to other nations and on the US civilian market. At times, these surplus T-6s had been sold for less than $500.00 each. The Air Force now had to repurchase a number of these aircraft with prices ranging as high as $8,000.00 each.

A total of 2,068 SNJ/T-6 airframes were remanufactured as T-6Gs. The Navy had planned a similar rebuild program and had scheduled to rebuild fifty early SNJs under the designation SNJ-7; however, in the event, only six were completed before the project was cancelled. Three of these number were fitted with tail hooks, becoming SNJ-7Cs. A final Navy contract to build 240 new production SNJ-8 aircraft (NA-198) was cancelled before production got underway.

The T-6G was finally phased out of the Air Force inventory during 1958. The final training flights for Navy SNJs occurred on 14 March 1958 at Barrin Field, Alabama. A number of T-6s, however, continued to serve with the Civil Air Patrol's 35th Air Rescue Squadron into the 1960s.

Three other Texan designations have appeared on the T-6 serial lists. The T-6H was a temporary designation assigned to Columbus-built T-6Gs. The T-6J was the designation assigned to 285 Canadian Car and Foundry-built Harvard Mk IVs bought with American aid money for use by the Mutual Defense Assistance Program (MDAP) to re-equip NATO air forces after the Second World War. These aircraft were supplied to France, West Germany, Italy, and Belgium.

Finally, there was the FT-6G — a one of a kind aircraft built in an attempt to sell the T-6 as a counter-insurgency (COIN) aircraft. The FT-6G was fitted with underwing pod-mounted .30 caliber machine guns and had provision for underwing rocket and bomb racks. Additionally, it could carry a fifty gallon external fuel tank or napalm tank on the fuselage centerline rack. Although never sold as a COIN aircraft, the FT-6G did contribute much toward the arming of other T-6 variants that were in service with such nations such as France, Portugal, Spain and Brazil, among others. Over the course of their careers, these armed T-6s served in the combat role during a number of small brush-fire wars — in some cases, being the only combat aircraft available.

The commander of the training school at Hondo AFB used this T-6G as his personal aircraft. The tip of the tail is in Red, Yellow and Blue representing the squadrons under his command. The T-6G had a reduced frame canopy and a football shaped direction-finding (DF) antenna housing behind the cockpit. (Dorr)

Canopy Development

AT-6F

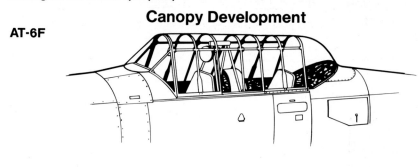

T-6G

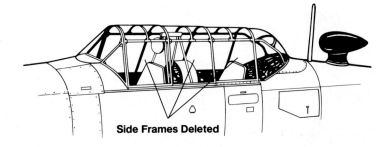

Side Frames Deleted

(Above) T-6Gs were issued to Air National Guard units for proficiency flying training. This colorful New Mexico Air National Guard T-6G is overall Trainer Yellow with Black and Light Yellow stripes on the tail, propeller spinner, and wheel covers. (Garrett)

(Below) A T-6G of California Air National Guard flies over Hayward, California during 1953. The T-6G featured dual rear position lights on the lower rudder and a football ADF housing behind the cockpit. The lettering under the center canopy reads: Instrument Aircraft - Aerobatics Prohibited. (Larkins)

SUSIE Q, a T-6G of the Pennsylvania Air Guard, now resides in the Air Force Museum at Dayton, Ohio. The Texan was stripped of its overall Yellow paint scheme and repainted in a pre-war trainer color scheme. The name was in Black with Red shading. (AFM)

39

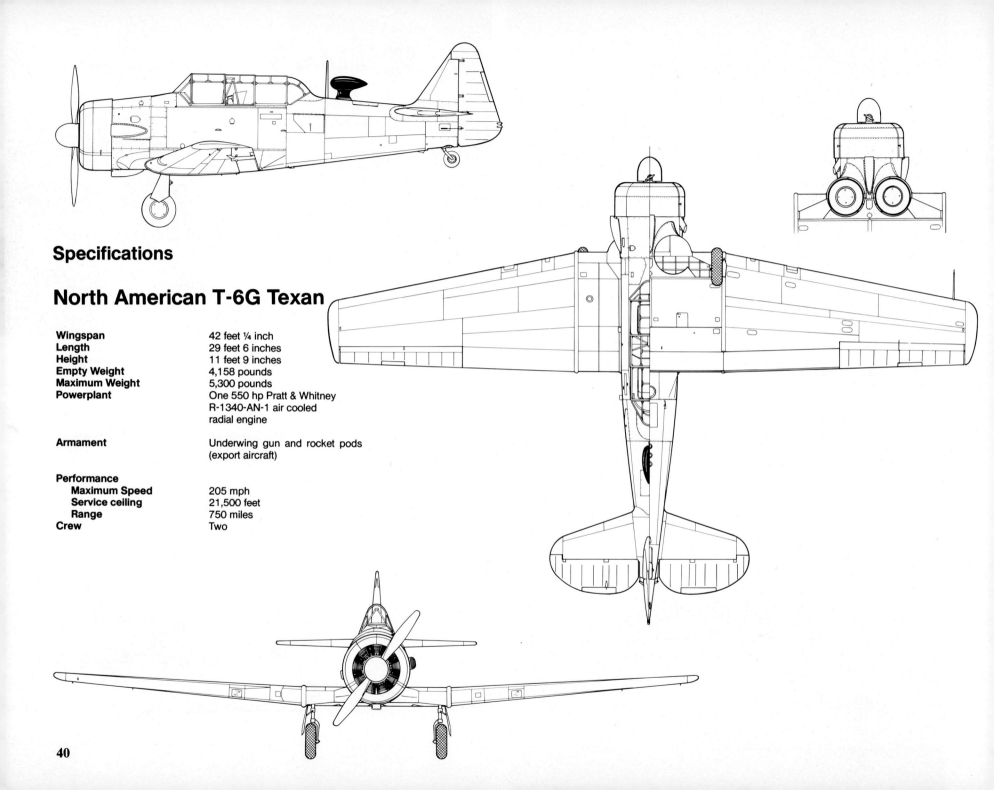

Specifications

North American T-6G Texan

Wingspan	42 feet ¼ inch
Length	29 feet 6 inches
Height	11 feet 9 inches
Empty Weight	4,158 pounds
Maximum Weight	5,300 pounds
Powerplant	One 550 hp Pratt & Whitney R-1340-AN-1 air cooled radial engine
Armament	Underwing gun and rocket pods (export aircraft)
Performance	
Maximum Speed	205 mph
Service ceiling	21,500 feet
Range	750 miles
Crew	Two

The USAF purchased 285 Harvard Mk IVs under the designation T-6J. The majority of the T-6Js were then exported to other nations under the MDAP program. The expanding European air forces of NATO received the majority of these T-6Js, although a few were retained by the USAF. (CCF via Dorr)

The West German *Bundesluftwaffe* received a number of CCF-built T-6Js (Harvard Mk IV) under the MDAP program. This T-6J Harvard was on display as part of a public open house at Buchel GAFB during July of 1960. (Menard)

The Spanish Air Force operated both the T-6G and Harvard IV as late as 1980. The T-6Gs and Harvard IVs were designated E.16 and a number were armed with wing guns and rockets for counter-insurgency (COIN) missions over the Spanish Sahara in North Africa. (G. Avila)

This T-6G (49-3538) was modified by North American for the counter-insurgency (COIN) role under the designation FT-6G. The aircraft mounted two .30 caliber machine gun pods under the wings and up to 400 pounds of ordnance on underwing racks. (Larkins)

Harvard Mk I

As the British began to establish the Empire Air Training Scheme, a massive pilot training program, they soon realized that trainer production in England would not be able to meet the demand for new aircraft. The British began seeking suitable aircraft in the United States and having been impressed with the North American Yale (BT-14), also evaluated the BC-1. The BC-1 more than met the British requirements and the British Purchasing Commission placed an order for an advanced trainer similar to the BC-1 under the designation Harvard Mk I.

The Harvard Mk I (NA-49) was basically a BC-1 outfitted with British specified equipment. It had the BC-1 fabric covered fuselage, retractable landing gear, rounded wingtips, and rounded rudder. It was powered, however, by a British specified 600 hp Pratt & Whitney R-1340-S3H1 in place of the 550 hp Pratt & Whitney R-1340-47 installed in the BC-1. Items of British specified equipment installed included a circular control column, British instruments and radios, and provision for a single .303 Vickers machine gun mounted in the right wing.

North American test pilot Louis Wait flew the first Harvard I (N7000) for the first time on 28 September 1938. Following acceptance by the British representatives at North American, the aircraft was shipped to England on 24 October, arriving at RAF Martlesham in December. The British purchasing commission had placed an initial order for 200 Harvard Mk Is. As these aircraft came off the assembly line, they were disassembled, crated, trucked to New York, and loaded aboard cargo ships making the convoy run to Great Britain. Upon arrival at the British assembly base at Shawbury, they were reassembled and test flown before being issued to a training unit.

Later, when the Royal Air Force relocated the majority of its training units to the United States and Canada, Harvards were flown directly from the factory to their assigned units. During January of 1939, the British placed a second order for an additional 200 Harvard Mk Is, while another order for thirty aircraft was placed on behalf of the Royal Canadian Air Force.

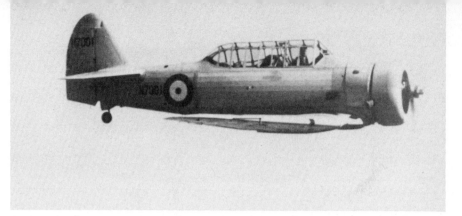

The second production Harvard I in flight over England during January of 1939. The Harvard Mk Is were initially assembled and test flown at North American, then disassembled and crated for shipment by sea to England. After arrival they were reassembled at Shawbury and test flown before being issued to a training unit. (IWM)

A flight of Harvard Mk Is of No 2 Flying Training Squadron over England during 1941. RAF training units were soon moved to Canada both to make room for combat aircraft airfields in England, and to provide safer conditions for the cadet training. (IWM)

The first production Harvard Mk I rolled out of the North American plant in September of 1938. The Harvard I was externally identical to the BC-1 and was equipped with British-specified equipment such as radios and a circular-grip control column. (NAA)

Wirraway

During 1936 a mission from the newly formed Commonwealth Aircraft Corporation of Australia visited North American to evaluate the NA-16 for possible production in Australia. Initially a single fixed landing gear NA-32 (BT-9) was imported to Australia for evaluation, followed by a single BC-1 (NA-33). A manufacturing license was negotiated under which Commonwealth Aircraft Corporation (CAC) was granted the rights to use the NA-33 as the basis for a general purpose aircraft to be built in Australia under the designation Wirraway (an aboriginal word meaning challenge).

The Wirraway was essentially a BC-1 with Australian specified modifications. The aircraft was fitted with a three blade propeller, twin .303 Vickers machine guns were mounted in the nose, a third .303 was mounted on a flexible mount in the rear cockpit, and underwing racks were installed for carrying up to 500 pounds of bombs. Although the Wirraway had the retractable landing gear BC-1 wing, it retained the rounded wingtips and rounded rudder of the BT-9 series. Commonwealth Aircraft rolled out the first production Wirraway during March of 1939 and the aircraft made its first official flight on 27 March. Deliveries of production Wirraways began during July of 1939 when the first three aircraft off the production line were turned over to the Royal Australian Air Force.

The Royal Australian Air Force used the Wirraway in every conceivable role during the early war years. Wirraways were pressed into service as interceptors and fighter-bombers, they were used for long range patrols, and as forward observer aircraft. Nos 21 and 24 Squadrons used Wirraways during the heavy action over New Guinea and Rabaul during the early days of the Pacific War.

The Wirraway is the only T-6 variant to be credited with a confirmed air-to-air kill in any war. On 26 December 1942 (Boxing Day), Flight Lieutenant John Archer and Sergeant N.J. Muir of No 4 Army Cooperation Squadron took off from Buna in Wirraway A20-103 on a reconnaissance mission of the Gona Wreck. The Japanese transport was lying off the Buna coast and earlier reports suggested that the Japanese were using it for radio relay and aircraft spotting. Soon after flying over the wreck, Archer spotted a lone Japanese Zero about 500 feet below him. Although, he knew that the Wirraway was no match for a Zero, Archer dove on the unsuspecting Japanese pilot. As soon as he was within range Archer opened fire with a short burst, then turned away, and ran for home. Looking back over his shoulder, Archer watched in great surprise as the Zero banked over and plunged into the sea. It was later discovered that a single round from Archer's guns had hit the Japanese pilot in the head, killing him instantly. It was quite an accomplishment for Archer to have shot down what was then regarded as the finest fighter aircraft in the Pacific Theater. For his heroic action Flight Lieutenant Archer was awarded the U.S. Silver Star. Two days after his victory, his Wirraway was painted with a small Japanese kill marking on the nose under the guns, — it carried this marking throughout the rest of the war.

After the war the Wirraway continued in service in the training role. During the Korean War, RAAF Wirraways performed various duties, including that of forward air controller, similar to the mission performed by USAF LT-6Gs. The Wirraway was continued in use by the RAAF as a trainer until it was finally retired during 1959. Commonwealth Aircraft Corporation built a total of 755 Wirraways.

During the early days of the Second World War, Commonwealth was called upon by the Australian government to develop a single seat fighter version of the Wirraway. At the time Australia had no first line fighters and the probability of quick reinforcements from Britain or the US was highly unlikely.

This RAAF Wirraway is camouflaged in Dark Earth and Foliage Green uppersurfaces with Aluminum undersurfaces. During the early days of the Pacific War, the Wirraway was pressed into service as a two seat fighter, fighter-bomber, and observation aircraft. One Wirraway pilot is credited with a kill, a Japanese Zero fighter. (IWM)

The fighter would be powered by the most powerful engine available in Australia, the 1,200 hp Pratt & Whitney R-1830-S34C-G radial engine. The aircraft featured a new fuselage (which used as many Wirraway parts as possible) mated with a somewhat shortened Wirraway wing, while the tail section was virtually unchanged. Given the name Boomerang, it was a true fighter armed with two 20MM cannons, four .303 machine guns, and racks for underwing bombs. The Boomerang was quite similar in appearance to the North American NA-50A/P-64. Boomerangs served with the RAAF throughout the war, mainly in the ground support and forward observer roles.

Australia purchased a manufacturing license for the NA-33 armed variant of the basic BC-1 during 1937. Commonwealth Aircraft Corporation built a total of 755 NA-33s under the designation CA-16 Wirraway. The Wirraway was armed with two Vickers .303 machine guns in the cowling, and a third .303 machine gun in the rear cockpit. (NAA)

This Royal Australian Air Force CA-16 Wirraway at RAAF Toluuwal during September of 1961 carries the post-war RAAF Kangaroo markings. Although rebuilt after the war and brought up to standards similar to those of the T-6G, the Wirraway retained its fabric-covered fuselage. (Dorr)

Sinbad II, a Commonwealth CA-13 Boomerang of No 5 Squadron Royal Australian Air Force during 1944. The Boomerang closely resembled the North American-designed P-64, and used a large amount of NA-16/Wirraway technology. It was armed with four .303 machine guns and two 20mm cannon. (AFM)

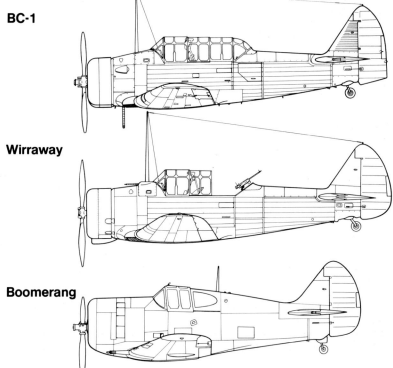

BC-1

Wirraway

Boomerang

44

Harvard II/III/IV

The Harvard Mk II (NA-66) was basically a BC-1A fitted with British equipment such as a circular RAF control column, British instrumentation and radios. British complaints about the cockpit heater led North American to install an extended exhaust shroud on the starboard side of the fuselage which routed warm air into the cockpit. This modification ended complaints about cockpit heating, and became one of the primary identification features for the Harvard series.

Harvard IIs also differed from the US BC-1/AT-6 in not having the tall antenna mast mounted in front of the windscreen which was common on American BC-1A/AT-6 aircraft. Armament was comprised of two .303 Vickers machine guns, one in the nose and a second gun in the rear cockpit. The aircraft were delivered from the factory finished in an overall Trainer Yellow paint scheme.

The British government ordered a total of 600 Harvard Mk IIs. Twenty aircraft for the RAF, sixty-seven for the Royal New Zealand Air Force, and 513 for the Royal Canadian Air Force; however, only 486 of the RCAF order were actually delivered. Later Britain ordered an additional 100 Harvard Mk IIs specifically for the RCAF. The French ordered 450 NA-76 aircraft (which were basically Harvard Mk IIs with French equipment and a tall antenna mast), just two weeks before the country fell to the Germans. All 450 aircraft on the French order were taken over by Great Britain. A further order for 125 Harvard Mk IIs was placed by the RAF in July of 1940. A number of these aircraft were taken over by the US Army Air Corps during 1940 when the US began building up toward a war footing.

Harvard Mk IIA/B

Harvard Mk IIAs (NA-88) were AT-6Cs that were obtained by the British through the Lend Lease program. Under Lend Lease, the RAF received a total of 747 Harvard Mk IIAs. These could be distinguished from the other Harvards in service with the RAF by the absence of the extended exhaust shroud and overall natural metal finish.

The Harvard Mk IIB was a BC-1A/AT-6A that was built under license by Noorduyn Aviation Ltd. in Montreal, Canada. These aircraft were built to RAF specification and did not have the long antenna mast. They were equipped with the extended exhaust shroud and were delivered in overall Trainer Yellow. Although Noorduyn had purchased the manufacturing license to the BC-1 during 1938, their first orders for the type were not received until January of 1940 when the Royal Canadian Air Force ordered 210 Harvard Mk IIBs. Following this order, the U.S. government ordered 1,500 Harvard Mk IIBs on behalf of the RCAF under the Lend Lease program. These aircraft received the U.S. designation AT-16 for paper work purposes. Shortly thereafter, the U.S. government ordered an additional 900 aircraft for the Royal Air Force. With orders totaling some 2,800 aircraft Noorduyn had to seek additional factory space and opened a second plant at Longue Pointe, Canada.

Harvard III

The Harvard Mk III (NA-88) was an AT-6D built for the Royal Air Force by North American. As with other T-6 variants coming off the Dallas production line at this time, the Harvard Mk IIIs were interspersed on the production line along side U.S. Army AT-6s and Navy SNJs. Twenty-five of the Harvard Mk III were in fact AT-6Ds (20) and SNJ-

Noorduyn Aviation in Canada built a total of 2,910 Harvard Mk IIBs for the RAF, RCAF, and U.S. Army Air Force (under the designation AT-16). The extended exhaust shroud was designed to feed heated air into the cockpit to increase cabin heat in cold weather. (Noorduyn via Larkins)

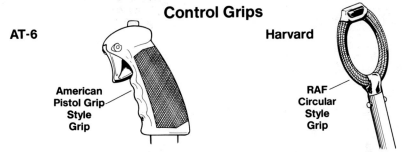

Control Grips

AT-6   Harvard

American Pistol Grip Style Grip

RAF Circular Style Grip

5s (5) that were delivered to the Royal Navy with U.S. equipment and RAF serial numbers. A total of 537 Harvard Mk IIIs were built, and among these there were a number that featured the formed plywood rear fuselage of the AT-6C/SNJ-4.

Harvard IV

During 1951 a program was initiated in Canada that was similar to that conducted by the U.S. Air Force with the T-6G. Under the U.S. program numerous T-6/SNJ airframes were rebuilt to T-6G specification. In Canada, entirely new aircraft were built, initially from left over spare parts. Canadian Car and Foundry, successor to Noorduyn Aviation, produced a total of 555 Harvard Mk IVs at its plant in Fort William, Quebec. The first forty aircraft off the production line were built from the spare parts/airframe inventory left over from Noorduyn. These were followed by another 515 being new production aircraft. The Harvard Mk IV had a reduced framed canopy, steerable tail wheel, increase fuel capacity, and updated radios, instruments, and hydraulic systems. Production began during 1951 and, of the 555 Harvard IVs built, 285 were purchased with U.S. Mutual Defense Assistance Program funds and furnished to various NATO air forces during the 1950s as T-6Js.

This Harvard Mk IIB of the Royal Canadian Air Force is painted overall Trainer Yellow. The aircraft is fitted with an extended exhaust shroud and two venturi tubes on the fuselage side above the exhaust. Unlike RAF Harvards, Noorduyn-built aircraft had American instruments and controls. (RCAF via Dorr)

A Harvard Mk II of the Royal Netherlands Air Force at Soesterberg Air Base in June of 1967. B-194 was originally an RAF aircraft (serial FS 661) passed on to the RNAF after the end of the Second World War. RNAF Harvards were camouflaged in overall Dark Green with the aircraft codes in White. (Bossenbrock via Taylor)

The Israeli Defense Force/Air Force had two Harvard Mk IIs that it used as fighter-bombers during the 1948 War of Independence. This weathered Harvard carries the fuselage number 1113 and tail number 13 and is camouflaged in Desert Tan and Olive Green uppersurfaces over Light Gray undersurfaces. Israeli Harvards also had Red cowlings and Yellow identification bands on the fuselage. (Taylor)

Swiss Air Force Harvards of an Operational Night Flying Training Unit parked on the grass at their home base. (Kyburz via Stapfer)

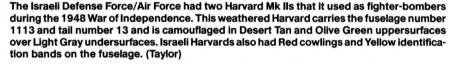

A trio of Harvard IIs of the Royal New Zealand Air Force based at Wigam, New Zealand. Harvard Mk IIs were built by North American alongside AT-6s and SNJs. The Harvard II in the foreground, NZ1085, was originally an RAF aircraft (serial EZ329). During construction the aircraft also carried the Army serial 42-84543. (Taylor)

Trailing smoke, a trio of RNZAF Harvard IIBs pull into a vertical climb at an airshow during the late 1950s. The excellent flying characteristics of the AT-6 made it a natural for the aerobatic role and many air forces throughout the world had Texan equipped aerobatic teams, including Brazil, Italy, and Canada.

Exhausts

AT-6

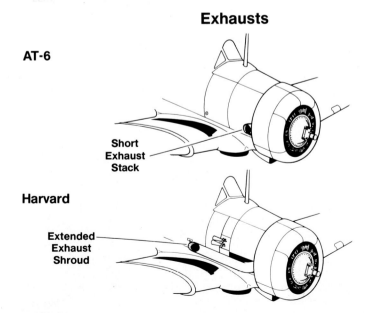

Short
Exhaust
Stack

Harvard

Extended
Exhaust
Shroud

This CCF-built Royal Canadian Air Force Harvard IIB has an unusually long exhaust shroud which extends back over the wing trailing edge. The aircraft was painted in overall Trainer Yellow with the cowling in Red. (Balogh)

The Canadian Car and Foundry company built 555 Harvard Mk IVs with production beginning during 1951. The Harvard IV was basically the RCAF version of the updated T-6G, with the addition of an extended exhaust shroud and a smaller ADF antenna housing behind the canopy. (Dorr)

A Harvard Mk IV of the RCAF during the 1950s. The Harvard is overall Trainer Yellow with a Black anti-glare panel and fuselage squadron codes. Canada operated large numbers of Harvards in the training role throughout the 1950s. (Balogh)

T-6s In Korea

Officially they were known as FACs — Forward Air Controllers, but to the men on the ground in Korea, both United Nations and Communist, they were known as the Mosquitoes. The men and aircraft of the 6147th Tactical Control Group were the eyes of the 5th Air Force during the Korean War.

During the Second World War there was no forward air control mission to speak of. Allied air forces had near total air superiority over Europe from just before D-Day through the end of the war and roaming packs of Allied fighter-bombers usually picked out their own targets of opportunity, or were directed from the ground. In Korea the situation was different. The United Nations fighter-bombers, mostly 5th Air Force and U.S. Navy jets, had to fly hundreds of miles from bases in Japan or from aircraft carriers in the Yellow Sea to reach the target area. Once in the target area they had only a few minutes to both find the target and attack it before their limited fuel supply forced them to return to base.

With the North Korean Communists closing in on Pusan, GEN Earl Partridge, 5th AF Commander, came up with the idea of using small, fast, light aircraft to locate the target, then guide the fighter-bombers onto the target so they would not waste valuable time and fuel. L-5 and L-19 spotter aircraft, however, were too slow and vulnerable to be used over North Korea. What was needed was a faster, more rugged, but readily available aircraft to fill this new mission. GEN Partridge found the aircraft he needed in the T-6 Texan. The Texans were fast enough, rugged enough, and they were available since at least one T-6 was assigned to every unit in the Korean theater.

The mission of the Airborne Tactical Air Controller was to conduct tactical reconnaissance of front line troop dispositions and activities along the main lines of enemy communications, control air strikes in the immediate vicinity of friendly troops, and control pre-briefed air strikes against designated targets. The mission was put in effect on 9 July 1950 when seven officers and three L-5G Stinson spotter aircraft began flying forward air control missions from Taejon in South Korea.

The next day, 10 July 1950, the first of the T-6s arrived; a T-6C which had been a derelict assigned to the 35th Fighter Interceptor Group in Japan. The Texan had been grounded for over a year due to other more pressing maintenance priorities. On orders from General Partridge, the T-6C was put back into flying status and equipped with an AN/ARC-3 radio set for communications with both the ground forces and the fighter-bombers. On the first day of T-6 operations, LT James Bryant and LT Frank Mitchell spotted a column of forty-two North Korean tanks on a road near Chochiwon. Bryant called in the waiting F-80C Shooting Star fighter-bombers who strafed and rocketed the tank column leaving seventeen tanks destroyed on the road.

The T-6s roamed the length and breadth of the Korean peninsula looking for any target worth shooting at — troops, tanks, trucks, trains, sampans; all fell prey to the FACs. On 15 July 1950, Headquarters 5th Air Force assigned the FAC unit its call sign, Mosquito. Each mission had a Mosquito call sign, from Mosquito Able through Mosquito How. Between this call sign and the distinctive sound of the Pratt & Whitney Wasp engine, the legend of the T-6 Mosquito was born. Even the Communists began referring to the unit as the Mosquito Squadron.

The unit was first assigned to the 6132nd Tactical Air Control Group, a support unit that had no aircraft or any organization for aircraft and pilots and no official status as a flying unit. The conditions of both the aircraft and crews rapidly deteriorated. The communists had forced the unit to relocate to Taegu inside the Pusan Pocket. Without an official unit designation, the squadron, now comprised of twenty-five men and twelve T-6s, was forced to beg, borrow, or steal virtually everything they needed just to stay alive. They lived in tents supplied by other units at Taegu; field equipment such as showers, kitchens, etc were unavailable so they bathed in the nearby river and ate C-rations. The entire base had only one latrine and very little toilet tissue. Despite these conditions, the Mosquito Squadron flew 269 sorties by the end of July. On 29 July 1950, Headquarters 5th AF "officially" activated the unit as the 6147th Tactical Control Squadron (Airborne) at Taegu, some three weeks after the unit had flown its first mission.

For the next four months the unit chased the North Koreans down and then back up the Korean peninsula. The month of August and half of September saw the Mosquitoes help stem the Communist advance and hold the Pusan Pocket. On 15 September GEN Douglas MacArthur's troops landed at Inchon, while units of the 8th Army, supported by 5th AF and Navy aircraft, broke out of the Pusan Pocket. By November of 1950, the Mosquitoes had moved first to Seoul City then to Pyongyang East, an airfield near the North Korean capitol. They had flown close air support missions over the front lines, deep penetration missions to watch for enemy troop buildups, search and rescue missions locating downed friendly pilots, leaflet-dropping missions, had flown VIPs and correspondents on briefing missions over the front line, and even night harassment missions. Later in the war they were even used as interceptors against the North Korean PO-2 biplane night raiders. Between 9 July and 25 November 1950, the 6147th TCS(A) flew a total of 4,902 combat sorties that resulted in the destruction of 436 tanks, 2,332 vehicles, 598 artillery guns, 1,045 villages housing enemy troops, 1,302 troop concentrations, 29 bridges, 8 locomotives, 101 rail cars, 228 supply dumps, 27 ammo dumps, and 98 fuel dumps. For their actions, the 6147th TCS was awarded two Distinguished Unit Citations.

With the Chinese intervention into the Korean War during November of 1950, the unit was forced to withdraw southward, first back to Seoul City, then further down the peninsula to Chunchon. Chunchon would become their permanent base of operations for the remainder of the war. The unit was now designated the 6147th Tactical Control

The Republic of Korea Air Force had two T-6Ds on strength (their most modern aircraft) when the North Koreans invaded during June of 1950. The aircraft survived the early fighting and continued to serve as trainers throughout the war. The aircraft in the background are camouflaged T-6Ds and Fs from the 6147th TCS(A). (Army)

The U.S. Navy used SNJs in Korea for utility work, flying commanders and VIPs to meetings, or taking press people out to the carriers. This SNJ-5C was assigned to the Joint Operations Center/Korea. The JOC was responsible for coordinating missions between Navy and 5th Air Force strike aircraft. (Reiling)

Group with three squadrons assigned; the 6148th and 6149th TCS (Airborne) flew the missions, while the 6150th TCS (Ground) handled ground support. The ground element also included front line ground forward air control teams. The 6150th TCS operated three-man teams, called Tactical Air Control Parties (TACP), that used radio equipped jeeps to call in air support aircraft all along the front lines. Each team consisted of a Mosquito pilot officer, a radio mechanic, and a vehicle mechanic. Their mission was to communicate with both the Mosquito airborne controllers and/or to radio relay aircraft flying nearby. They could also call in fighter-bombers themselves if they were within radio range. Every new Mosquito pilot was required to serve sixty days with a ground team. With two squadrons of aircraft and crews available, the units were able to divide Korea between them, with the 6148th covering the western sector and the 6149th the eastern portions. At least one Mosquito was kept airborne over each sector during daylight hours.

It was during this period that the unit began receiving new aircraft; re-manufactured T-6G aircraft purpose-built for their mission. These aircraft were designated as LT-6Gs and differed in several ways from trainer T-6Gs. First the aircraft were brought up to T-6G standards, then they were modified for the FAC mission with the AN/ARC-3, AN/ARN-6, and SCR-522A radios which allowed for communications with almost everyone in Korea. The aircraft were armed with six underwing racks carrying triple rocket launchers and two .30 caliber machine guns mounted in pods carried under the wings. The guns were later removed when the pilots decided that extra speed was more desirable than the firepower of the .30 caliber guns. Ninety-nine LT-6Gs were built for the Mosquito mission all identified by a 'L' being added to the aircraft's buzz number (such as LTA-XXX). A total of ninety-seven LT-6Gs were produced.

A T-6F of the 6147th TCS(A) at Taegu during the Summer of 1950. The 6147th crews liked the T-6F over other variants since the F variant could carry a belly tank. The extra fuel added to their loiter time over the target area. The cowling is Yellow, the wings have White center panels with Red stripes, and the tail is Red. (Eubank via Taylor)

The mission of the 6147th Tactical Control Squadron (Airborne) was low-level reconnaissance at or near the front lines in Korea. This T-6D was damaged by a cable stretched between two mountains, and force-landed at K-24 (Pyongyang) in October of 1950. The Red stripes on the upper wings were a recognition aid. (McGettigan via Mosquito Assn.)

With the war on the ground at a virtual stalemate, the role of the Mosquitoes shifted to location of enemy troop assembly and buildup areas, and long range recon missions along known supply routes. Every once in awhile a really outstanding mission would take place. During the Summer of 1951 LT Dick Meade was jumped by a North Korean Yak-9 fighter over the front lines . Meade went into an ever-tightening Lufberry circle until he eventually ended up behind the Yak. With no other offensive armament available to him, Meade salvoed all his smoke rockets at the Yak. Although the rockets missed, he must have scared the hell out of the Yak driver, who immediately broke off the combat and fled North. On 15 July 1953 LT Sydney Johnson and his TACP team observed some 10,000 Chinese troops advancing through the Kumsong valley straight at them, in broad daylight! Johnson called for help and was answered by three squadrons of F-84 Thunderjets and three squadrons of F-86F Sabres. Over the course of the day each of the fighter-bombers flew at least eight missions against the Chinese troops. Some of the fighter pilots did not shut down their engines while re-arming, trying to get the fastest turn around possible. When it was all over, an entire Chinese Regiment had been decimated.

By the end of the Korean War the 6147th TCG had accumulated a most enviable record. They had flown 40,354 sorties totalling 117,471 combat hours. They had been instrumental in the destruction of at least eight communist divisions, knocked out at least five tank divisions, 563 artillery pieces, 5,079 vehicles, 12 locomotives, untold thousands of rail cars, and 84 bridges. The Mosquitoes lost thirty-three men and forty-two aircraft which were either shot down or written off due to battle damage.

This Yellow cowled T-6F is armed with six 2.5 inch smoke rockets and is carrying a fifty-five gallon belly drop tank. Early in the war the aircraft assigned to the 6147th TCS carried a variety of markings, most of which were leftovers from their previous units. (Eubanks via Taylor)

Sometimes the T-6s of the 6147th were called on for duties other than reconnaissance. These Black and Yellow checkered cowl T-6Ds are used for Mosquito spraying — a Mosquito spraying for Mosquitoes. The large underwing spray tanks had nozzles under them which controlled the amount of DDT sprayed. (USAF)

Both South Korean and U.S. airmen serviced the T-6s of the 6147th TCS during the war. The Koreans needed the training and the 6147th ground crews needed all the help they could get in keeping the T-6s combat ready. This T-6D has been modified with a belly tank installation. (Mosquito Assn.)

51

A 6148th TCS T-6 Mosquito flies low over a 6150th Tactical Air Control Party jeep. Every 6147th TCG pilot served sixty days in a TACP jeep, operating along the front lines with the ground troops before flying his first combat mission. (USAF)

The harsh Korean winters caused problems for the air cooled engines of the T-6s, so the 6147th crews installed local manufactured engine covers inside the cowling front to keep the engines warm. (Mosquito Assn.)

This T-6 at K-47 (Chunchon) during 1951 is armed with two underwing .30 caliber machine gun pods. The gun pods were usually removed to lighten the aircraft and improve performance. Additionally, senior officers did not want the FAC pilots engaging targets themselves instead of calling in strike aircraft. (Mosquito Association)

This AT-6D Texan of the 6147th TCS at K-47 during 1951 has been stripped of its fuselage skin in preparation for undergoing intermediate maintenance. (Mosquito Association)

A fully armed LT-6G on the Chunchon ramp during 1953 ready for its next mission. The aircraft is fitted with multiple rocket launchers, a TACAN blade antenna behind the canopy, and another antenna mast between the landing gear wells. Wingtip and fin colors are Red, White, and Blue for the 6148th TCS(A). (NAA)

MOAN N' LISA, was named because of the strange sounds that came from the air flow over the many patches in her skin. The LT-6G was flown by LT Gene Risedorph out of Chunchon during 1953. LT-6Gs were specially modified and armed T-6Gs built for the Mosquito mission in Korea. (Risedorph)

LT-6G Armament

Smoke Rocket Installation

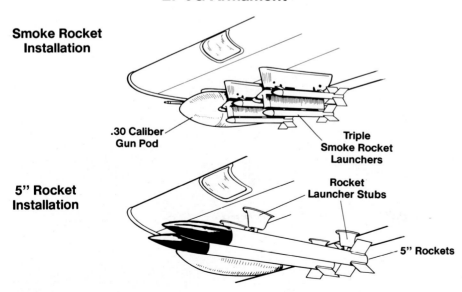

.30 Caliber Gun Pod

Triple Smoke Rocket Launchers

5" Rocket Installation

Rocket Launcher Stubs

5" Rockets

NIGHT TRAIN, an LT-6G of the 6149th TCS(A) flies formation with another LT-6 over Korea during 1953. Initially the LT-6Gs were armed with underwing .30 caliber machine gun pods, however, the aircrews usually had them removed to lighten the aircraft giving it added speed and a better rate of climb. (Mosquito Assn.)

An LT-6G of the 6148th TCS(A) on the pierced steel plank ramp at K-47, Chunchon, home of the Mosquitoes during 1953. The LT-6G could be fitted with multiple launchers and carry up to eighteen 2.5 inch smoke rockets or six 5 inch smoke rockets. The pilot, Casey Cameron, is reloading his only defensive armament, a Colt .45 automatic. (Cameron via Mosquito Assn.)

COL Watson, commander of the 6148th TCS(A), watches as one of his crews prepares to start the engine on this LT-6G (49-3556) named *Peggy*. The Mosquito Group lost forty-seven aircraft and thirty-three men to both combat and operational accidents during the Korean War. (Mosquito Assn.)

The ROK Navy's first aircraft was this T-6 floatplane. The 6147th T-6F ran out of gas and crash landed at Kwangju in December of 1950. ROK and US crews hauled the wreck to Chinhae where they modified it with the center float from a Japanese Rufe and wing tip floats made from F-80 tip tanks. It was known as the KN-1. (USAF)

Texans at War

Armed T-6s and Harvards have served in a number of brush-fire wars around the world. Armed Harvards were flown by the Israeli Defense Force/Air Force (IDF/AF) during the 1948 War of Independence, often against Syrian Air Force armed T-6s (the SAF operated some twenty armed AT-6s). During the 1956 Sinai Campaign, Israeli Harvards, now armed with anti-tank rockets and bombs, flew combat missions against Egyptian armored forces.

The Royal Air Force used armed Harvards against Communist terrorists in Malaysia during 1948-1951 and again against Mau-Mau terrorists in Kenya during 1952-1960.

The French Air Force used various models of the Texan/Harvard, modified for the counter-insurgency role, during the Algerian campaign (1954 through 1961). T-6Gs, Harvards, and a number of ex-Navy SNJs were modified with underwing gun pods mounting dual 7.5MM machine guns, and racks for bombs, rockets, and napalm tanks. Later the French T-6s, known as Tomcats, were modified to carry 100 litre napalm tanks, and rocket pods. Several different types of pods were carried, such as the eighteen or thirty-six 36MM rocket pod, or seven-shot 68MM rocket pods.

By 1958, the French *Armie de L'Air Algerie* had some thirty squadrons of armed T-6/Harvard aircraft available for use against the guerrilla forces. The French began phasing out the T-6 Tomcat in favor of the much more powerful, faster North American T-28 Fennec during 1959. During the early 1960s, the French government sold large numbers of their veteran T-6s to other nations.

Belgium used armed Harvards and T-6s in the Congo in the counter-insurgency role. Later, a number of these aircraft would be transferred to the newly formed Congolese Air Force and would see action again during the Congolese civil war.

During the 1960s, the armed T-6 was the mainstay of the Portugese Air Force effort in Africa against rebels in Angola, Mozambique, and Portugese Guinea. Armed with gun and rocket pods, the Texans were used in the counter-insurgency role until Portugal finally gave up her African colonies in August of 1974.

A number of armed T-6Gs were flown in Laos and Cambodia against Viet Cong targets along the Ho Chi Minh Trail during the Vietnam War.

Several ex-French aircraft flew combat once again over Biafra during the Nigerian Civil War (1967-1970) and are credited with destroying at least one Nigerian Air Force MiG-17 Fresco fighter on the ground.

Spain used modified T-6s against guerrillas in North Africa. Spanish Air Force T-6s were modified with a .30 caliber machine gun mounted in each wing and underwing racks for bombs and rockets. On one mission during 1975, a Spanish pilot reportedly came face to face with one of the most modern air defense weapons when his E.16 (T-6G) had a pair of Soviet-made SA-7 Strella shoulder-fired, heat-seeking missiles fired at him over the Sahara. The pilot successfully evaded the missiles and his wingmen blasted the launch site. However, it was evident that the T-6's time as a combat aircraft had come to an end.

Today the Texan soldiers on with many smaller nations, especially in Central and South America. Besides being used in the training role, a number of these are flown in the Counter-Insurgency and armed-reconnaissance roles despite the threat from shoulder fired missiles. The T-6, however, cannot be expected to survive in a hostile environment where modern air defense technology is present — after all, the Texan is a trainer!

A French Air Force T-6G of 5/72 Ground Support Light Squadron (EALA) flies over Algeria during the late 1950s. The French used armed T-6s and Harvards for missions against Algerian guerrilla forces. French T-6s had underwing .30 caliber gun pods, and racks for bombs and/or rockets, a direct result of the FT-6G program. (Bertrand)

A French pilot alongside his T-6G in Algeria. The Texan is armed with rocket and gun pods. French T-6s were known as Tomcats and flew the majority of French combat missions from 1955 through 1961. They were later retired in favor of the faster and better armed North American T-28 Fennec. (Demasson)

Spanish Air Force C.6 (T-6C/D) and E.16 (T-6G) flew armed anti-guerrilla missions over the Spanish Sahara desert provinces during the 1970s. Spanish aircraft were armed with .30 caliber machine guns in both wings, and underwing racks for rockets and bombs. (Luenco)

An armed T-6G Texan of the Portugese Air Force on a strike mission over Angola. The Portugese used a number of armed Texans and Harvards for counter-insurgency missions in all their African possessions until 1974. (USAF)

Armament Options

5" Rockets

4 Rocket Stubs

36mm Or 68mm Rocket Pods

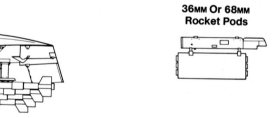

This camouflaged T-6 of the Brazilian Air Force is fitted with underwing racks for rockets and/or small bombs. The Brazilians used large numbers of T-6s, both in the training role and for counter-insurgency operations. (D. Hagedorn)

Twin 7.5mm Gun Pods

Front View

Side View

Bottom View

Bomb Racks

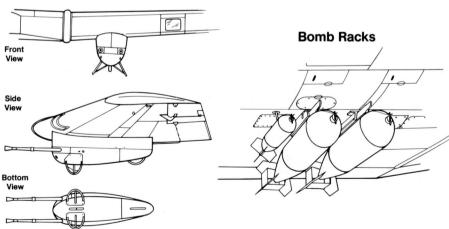

56

Civil T-6s

The popularity of the T-6 among private pilots has always been high. The aircraft is easy to maintain and operate, yet gives the private pilot a taste of high performance. So popular is the T-6 in the civilian community, that an organization devoted to restoring and flying the Texan was formed. The T-6 Owners Association along with Warbirds of America sponsor regular T-6 safety, maintenance, and operation seminars. Included on the U.S. civil register are twelve SNJ-2s, twenty-two AT-6As, seventy-three AT-6C/SNJ-4s, eighty-two AT-6D/SNJ-5s, sixty-eight AT-6F/SNJ-6s, three SNJ-7s, six Harvard Mk IIs, ten Harvard Mk IVs, and over one hundred T-6Gs.

The T-6 has its own racing catagory at the National Air Races in Reno, Nevada and is classified as an antique aircraft by the Experimental Aircraft Association (in the Warbird class). It is a rare airshow in the United States that does not have at least one T-6 on display. The numbers of T-6/Harvards active in Europe have also increased over the last few years, with Texans appearing on the civil registers of England, Spain, Italy, Sweden, Switzerland, Holland, Norway, and France.

Civil T-6s have been modified in a number of interesting ways, including one aircraft that was rebuilt with tricycle landing gear, bubble canopy, and wingtip fuel tanks. Known as the Bacon Super T-6S, the aircraft was built by Gordon Israel during 1957 and had a cruising speed of 216 mph (some forty-six mph faster than a stock T-6).

Other T-6s became movies stars, serving as the basis for the Zero fighters and Kate torpedo bombers in the movie "Tora, Tora, Tora." The Zeros were rebuilt with new cowlings, canopies, rudders, modified wing tips, and other parts to become rather accurate replicas of the famous Japanese fighter.

From the number of T-6s that remain active, it is likely that the Texan will be an active part of the civil community well into the next century, over sixty years from the NA-16 prototype's first flight.

Painted to resemble a Soviet Yak fighter for a movie, the Bacon Super T-6S takes off from Chino Air Port in California. The T-6S was a private attempt to sell remanufactured T-6s modified with new power plants, a bubble canopy, tricycle landing gear, and wingtip fuel tanks for the COIN role. (Larkins)

Hugh Alexander flew this T-6 Texan named *STEWBALL* as a pylon racer on the air race circuit. T-6s now have their own racing class at the National Air Races held in Reno, Nevada. (Larkins)

A number of T-6s were modified with new canopies, cowlings, rudders, and other parts for movie roles as Japanese Zeroes in the film "Tora, Tora, Tora." A number of these same aircraft were later used in the TV series "Black Sheep Squadron."

Other North American Aviation Aircraft From
squadron/signal

1034

1045

1089

squadron/signal publications